• Theories of Organization

• Theories of Organization

Henry L. Tosi
Michigan State University

St. Clair Press
4 East Huron Street
Chicago 60611

To Rosemary

Library of Congress Catalog Card Number 75-17063
ISBN 0-914292-02-1

First printing, September 1975
Second printing, April 1976
Third printing, February 1977

St. Clair Press
4 East Huron Street
Chicago, Illinois 60611

Contents

Preface

A book like this is—of course—never complete, and I take full responsibility for omitting some works that others would certainly agree should be included. But that is a matter of taste, which is why some of us prefer Bordeaux to Burgundy or Picasso to Miro.

These summaries, extracts, and reviews have been gathered from a number of sources. It is my hope that they present the major variables and interrelationships of the various points of view about organizational theory. The elegance and logic of the originals may have been lost, but I hope not the substance.

The purpose of this collection is to expose the student quickly to a broad range of theories. It is not meant to be a substitute for the complete works themselves. The student has too much to learn by immersing himself in the originals. I would have it no other way.

Henry L. Tosi

1 Introduction

Theory and Organizational Theory

> At present [those interested in organizations are] confronted with a situation in which numerous fragments of theories are presented as complete theories. . . . The systems developed [by the various schools of thought] are likely to consist of widely different variables that are really important to an organization (32:3).*

A cursory reading of several organizational theory texts will lead most of us to a conclusion consistent with Stogdill's, as given above. The intent of this book is to present a selection of the different theories, and attempt to delineate their skeletal structure, in the hope that thereby points of similarity and distinction may emerge and that thus other theoretical efforts can be devoted to refining those points. The theories presented in this book were selected because they are representative of certain approaches, have been widely used as point of reference, attack and/or present a formulation of an aspect of organization of particular interest to the present writer. The approaches have been condensed or summarized, or presented in some other brief form to show how the various elements within each theory are related to other elements. The selections are abstracts and represent what someone, generally other than the theorists, believes to be the main set of ideas and concepts in the particular theory. In the original work, the theorist usually marshals support for the concepts and ideas either by extensive reference to empirical research literature, as Stogdill (32) does, or from his own observations, as does Barnard (2). It is the responsibility of the serious student of theory to examine all theories in detail, so that he becomes aware of the bases for relationships as developed by the theorist.

The formulations presented here by no means exhaust the approaches to the study of organization. Stogdill, for example, has categorized no less than 18 orientations which have been used in the analysis of organizations. Among these are viewing an organization as a cultural product, or as an exchange agent with environment, or as an independent agency, or as a

*Numbered references will be found in the references at the back of this book.

system of structures and functions, or as a structure in action over time, or as a system of dynamic functions, or as a processing system, or as an input-output system, or as a structure of subgroups.

Additionally, some theories of organized behavior focus on groups. They may emphasize groups as biological social necessities, or as cultural products, or as independent entities, or as an interaction in systems, or as interaction-expectation systems, or as a collection of individual members, or as a summation of member characteristics.

Finally, subgroups may be the central anaytical unit, with the focus on subgroups in interaction with the organizations, or as in interaction with each other.

Each of these orientations represents a legitimate point of departure for inquiry, each has a different set of biases and value judgments which affect the manner in which the theory is developed, yet each focuses on organized behavior.

What is organization?

Every organizational theory has at least two possible aspects which tend to confuse (14). It either examines the process of subdividing work and work relationships into manageable units, or it may have a greater behavioral emphasis, concerned with the examination and analysis of relatively complex, structured behavior systems.

Conceptually, there are only slight differences in the way in which various theorists define organizations. Barnard (2) calls an organization a "system of consciously coordinated personal activities or forces," a "system of interrelated activities." Davis (8) defines it as "group of people working together, under a leader, to accomplish an objective." Victor Thompson (35) characterizes bureaucracy as "a highly rationalized impersonal integration of a large number of specialists operating to achieve some objective, upon which is superimposed a highly elaborate structure of authority." Stogdill (32) defines the organization as a "structured" system of behavior, with the position and roles comprising it having the potential of being "prestructured," that is, designed and prescribed before the roles are filled by actors.

Yet, while the various definitions do not seem radically different from each other, the directions taken, the concepts used, and the relationships between them is varied. But the object of study is still the same—the large complex organization. The characteristics of these large complex organizations are presented in detail within the various theory discussions later, but some are briefly noted here to provide a frame of reference for those discussions.

Large size is an implicit characteristic. In general, organizations treated in theory are of such a size that within them it is extremely difficult, if not impossible, to maintain close interpersonal relationships with a large number of the members, relative to the total membership.

Formalization derives partially from the large size of the organization and the need for some kind of control structure. Guidelines become necessary to provide a basis for the different kinds and types of interactions required between members since the size of the organization makes it extremely difficult for members to work these out among themselves on any other basis. Formalization simply means that procedures and policies are written and stated in such a way that they become stable, quasi-permanent directions, ranging from very general to very specific, for interaction and decisions. Formalization generally refers to written, documented guides for action and behavior of members and is common to all bureaucracies. It provides a degree of stability to interaction patterns, regardless of the incumbent of the position in the organization. Thus, when an individual newly arrives in an organization, there are specified actions and interactions which facilitate his learning.

Rationality is another attribute sought by large organizations. The purpose of imposing a structure is to bring order to a system of activities intended to achieve a goal. The system should be ordered on the basis of "logic and science." The activities of the members should be directed toward the goal. If activities are goal-directed, then resources can be more effectively utilized. Rationality is partially achieved by "goal factoring." The organization has a general goal. This goal is factored, or broken down into subgoals. These are assigned to lower-level units. If these units achieve their purpose or goal, the general organization goal will be attained. Individuals in lower-level units essentially "assume" the goal of the unit when they accept a position. They have an obligation to achieve their goals. These obligations may be viewed as "responsibilities of the position." In addition to the obligation, an incumbent will have certain prerogatives to allocate organization resources to accomplish these subunit goals. These prerogratives are often called "authority."

Hierarchical structure is therefore related to the nature of the factored goals. Hierarchy is the existence of different degrees of authority at the various levels of the organization. It is the chain of formal authority relationships from the top of the structure to its bottom, tying different levels of the organization together. The degree of authority at a particular level may be defined in terms of the range of discretion an individual has over resource allocation, both physical and human. In general, individuals in higher positions tend to have greater discretion and are accorded more status and deference than those at lower levels. It is through the authority structure that the various activities of the organization are tied together in order to achieve some degree of coordination in attaining goals.

Specialization is another dimension of the complex organization. Specialization refers to the particular grouping or configuration of activities performed *by an individual.* The range of activities assigned to a particular position, or individual, should be "rationally" grouped in such a way as to make sense in terms of effectiveness and efficiency. Specialization may be one of two types. First, it may refer to the *division of labor.* The particular task is analyzed and broken down into subtasks, which are its primary components. An individual then is assigned to perform these subtasks, which are essentially simpler and more repetitive than the total task requirements required to achieve a result. The individual is able to learn the tasks quickly and also its concomitant skills. This leads to both increased "efficiency" and less reliance by the organization on the skills of a particular person. Hence, personnel replacement is facilitated and relatively simple.

The second type of specialization has been called *social specialization* by Victor Thompson (35). This is the case where the person, not the work, is specialized. It means that the individual possesses a type or range of skills that cannot be routinized, either because of their complexity and intensive development, or because they are not needed in the great quantity that other more routine tasks are.

Theory and "organization theory"

The materials in the chapters that follow are generally called "theories of organization." They are attempts to present a systematic view of organized systems, or some dimensions of them, by developing various concepts which define elements of organization and how these are related to each other and to the "output" of organization.

Yet it may be presumptuous to use the term "theory" in a scientifically appropriate sense. Rudner (27) defines a theory as a "systematically related set of statements, including some law-like generalization that is empirically testable . . . [and] . . . the sort of systematic relatedness is deductive relatedness." Perhaps it would be better to call these organization theories "formulations." Some formulations may be theoretic while others should more correctly be called nontheoretic.

Theoretic systems. The use of the term "theory" in the phrase "organization theory" does not quite square with its meaning to the philosopher of science. Before a set of concepts is called a theory, certain requirements must be met (27).

The concepts, which form the language system of the theory, must be *observational*, or experimental. That is, they must be such that their existence can be verified through examination of the phenomena. These concepts are formed, related to each other, and used in the deductive process based upon a set of rules, which are also part of the theory.

Axioms, or givens, in the theoretical system are stable relationships between concepts which the theorist uses as a base from which to draw conclusions and inferences. The axioms, and a set of transformation rules, permit derivations and deductions to be made from the initially selected set of concepts.

Nontheoretic formulations. These are formulations which do not meet the requirements of theory noted above. They fall into two groups, definitional system and analytical schema. A definitional system contains a set of statements which consist of a term and an attendant definition. An analytical schema, on the other hand,

> includes over and above its system of definitions a set of analytic, or logically true or truistic sentences. These are truistic not by reference

to . . . empirical evidence, but by recourse to the systems definitions (27:31).

These nontheoretic systems are useful to the social scientist in that they may ultimately become part of a theory.

Rudner notes that it "would probably be fair to say that the vast preponderance of all formulations constituting the output of social scientists consist of such nontheoretic formulations as mentioned above." If so, how does the term "organization theory" apply? Strictly speaking, it doesn't. But, there has been a general application of that label to formulations which deal with the organization phenomenon. This convention, then, is followed and the formulations presented here are, by our definition, called "organization theories."

The bias of the theorist

All social science theory is composed of both "systematic and doctrinal elements which are embedded in its language, logical tools, concepts, empirical relationships and normative considerations. . . . However, the systematic character of a theory is rarely explicit, since it is usually hidden in matters of substance. But in the systematic elements that circumscribe theories of the business firm reside some of the crucial factors that determine and pattern vision of the firm" (14). The concepts and variables which are the building blocks of theory contain implicit biases and assumptions which may escape those who use the theory.

The theorist builds his system by defining, with some degree of precision, the variables which he includes. The values, beliefs, and background of the theorist tend to provide a limit of sorts on what these variables are. This is the "normative structure" of the theory (14). The theorist selects those variables which he believes, from general or empirical observation, are those which explain the system and/or are most amenable to control or change. This determines not only the variables and concepts which make up the theory, but also the manner in which they may be used to predict and explain. Whether or not a given phenomena may be studied in the laboratory, in a field experiment, or simply by observation is largely a function of the extent to which the researcher is capable of, or perhaps willing to operationalize concepts from a theory and/or the degree to which he is willing to interpret results from a "controlled" experiment into generalized effects that would occur in a "real world" environment.

Uses of theory

The purpose of theory is to "explain and predict." Rubenstein and Haberstroh (26) believe that "useful theories of organization should help us to: explain [and] observe organization behavior. . . predict future organizational behavior. . . [and]. . . influence future organizational behavior."

Theory has some value when it has *utility* and this may be prescriptive or descriptive. Some approaches to organization, especially those which

Krupp (14) has called "designed theory," present normative prescriptions about what conditions and relationships *should* exist in organizations. How should work be organized? How should authority and responsibility be assigned? What are the "principles" that should be complied with? Design theory has value in development and prescription of organizational relationships prior to the entrance of an individual into the system. It can throw up a "red flag," suggesting that when prescriptions are violated, problems *may* develop.

Design theory, then, has a sort of predictive aspect to it. For instance, the "traditional" concept of unity of command would lead to a general prediction of role conflict if violated. Obviously, however, there are conditions where role conflict may be less likely to occur. Theories which specify these conditions may have greater explanatory capability, but may be less effective in the design of an organization since consideration of *all* the variables would result in a complex construction extremely difficult to deal with.

Those theories which Krupp (14) has called "organization behavior" are directed to the *explanation* of behavior in organizations and tend to treat individual reactions to different degrees of behavioral prescription, or organization structure. These focus on human variables affected by structural considerations. Both design and organization behavior theory, or descriptive and prescriptive approaches, have the fundamental goal of understanding why, and what, things occur as they do in organizations.

Theory should also serve as the basis for research. The propositions and hypotheses which are explicit and implicit in theory provide guides and directions for empirical efforts toward verification or rejection of the theory itself, or its important hypothetical substructures. Rigby notes the use and importance of theory in research.

> Theory, including principles and laws, does not provide information on the state of the world, but only on the nature of the world. The applied researcher is . . . primarily interested in the state of the world. Theory . . . will suggest . . . how he can proceed to study the state of the world. . . . [It] provides . . . a set of concepts and information on the relationship between concepts.
>
> Applied research based in theory is in strong contrast to problem-solving research based on nothing more than simple trial and error or uncritical imitation.
>
> The role that theory can play in aiding applied research may seem obvious, but . . . is too frequently ignored in applied research. (25:65-67).

Bits and pieces of theories, adequately investigated, will serve to sharpen the explanatory and predictive capacity of theory. Dill (9) emphasizes this point by stressing the importance of:

> the replication of studies which have found their way into some theoretical structures. In a few areas we have done replications with highly beneficial results. The early experiments on participative manage-

ment . . . draw dramatic attention because of their apparently solid demonstration of the immediate practical benefits of participation. . . . Yet in each case . . . elaborations of the original experiment . . . have found that the simple relationships which they first hypothesized between participation, satisfaction, and productivity do not hold up . . . . As a result . . . we are reopening many old questions to establish more clearly the conditions under which these methods will and will not work (9:50-51).

Organization theory and other theory types

Probably one of the main reasons for the confusion among, and criticism of each other by, those who support various approaches to organization theory is an inability to agree on what it is.

It is sufficient to say here that organization theory is a set of interrelated constructs (concepts), definitions, and propositions that present a systematic view of behavior of individuals, groups, and subgroups *interacting* in some relatively patterned sequences of activity, the intent of which is goal-oriented.

Most would agree with this definition. But when we must decide whether or not a set of constructs should be called organization theory—or something else—a problem usually emerges. Very well. Another approach can be suggested. Is it possible to present some parameters which would allow us to determine what *is not* organization theory?

Management theory and organization theory. Stodgill (32) differentiates between organization theory and management theory. "A theory of organization is not necessarily a theory of management." While management theory must be based on organization theory, it contains *"philosophical assumptions and value orientations regarding the nature of human behavior that are not basic to a theory of organization."* Stodgill says that

> a theory of management is a theory of practice . . . interested in facts and sound principles. But theories of practice regarding human nature and human relations almost always involve schools of thought that differ in their philosophical orientations. The disputes between social scientists and classical theories are concerned with differences in recommended practice. . . . [While] these differences are significant for the practice of management, they do not affect any of the realities regarding the dimensions of organization. It is argued that organization theory is an instrument not for conducting ideological dispute but for acquiring verifiable knowledge (32:51).

This distinction may provide a basis for the resolution of some of the conflict between different theorists. Organization theory is descriptive and/or predictive. It is concerned with what an organization *is* and what will occur under certain kinds of structural or structural-interpersonal arrangements. It tells us what is and/or what will be. *It does not tell us what to do.* Organization theory, then, may be described as a set of related statements, hypotheses, etc., about (1) a set of variables which describe the parameters of organization, and perhaps organization behavior, and/or (2) a series of "if. . . then" statements which *predict* the effect of certain structural arrangements on performance and behavior.

Once the theorist reaches this point, of course, he must indeed find it easy to enter into the domain of management theory. Management theory is a "theory of practice." It must *prescribe* what to do to achieve a *particular* outcome, or to prevent a condition from developing which might be considered an undesirable. These prescriptions have manipulation or change as their intent. When these results are intended it is easy to provoke controversy and argument, since personal values come into consideration. *Management theory is best conceived of as a series of "if. . . then" statements to which are added "therefore, do. . ."* This argues, then, that approaches to organizational problems such as those of Taylor, Likert, Argyris, and McGregor which suggest a "better" way to organize or which describe how to manage "more effectively" should be characterized as management theories since they tend to be largely prescriptive in nature.

Organization theory and the "theory of the firm." McGuire (20) describes the major components of economic theory, or the "Theory of the Firm," as follows:

1) The firm has a goal (or goals) toward which it drives.
2) It moves toward [them] in a "rational" manner.
3) The firm's function is to transform economic inputs to outputs.
4) The environment within which the firm operates is given.
5) The theory concentrates particularly upon changes in the price and quantities of inputs and outputs.

With the exception of the last point, the list is similar to attributes of organization generally implied, or made explicit, in most theories of organization. For instance, in our earlier survey of definitions of organization we found that most included some sort of "goal orientation."

What, then, is the difference? First, the external environment with which the firm is concerned in economic theory is the "market." In some organization theories the treatment of the environment includes external interest and pressure groups which are not "customers." Selznick (30) treats the "community" in *TVA and the Grass Roots*. March and Simon point out that while they are structuring their theoretical formulation around decisions made by those normally viewed as organization members, one may well use the same kind of analysis for other groups, such as "customers." Second, the focal point in economic theory tends to be factor prices and quantities—or supply and demand. The following states nicely the distinction between organization theory and economic theory intended here:

> Formal economic analysis simplifies the empirical properties in the firm and molds it into a body of theory . . . . Organization theory looks at the internal characteristics of the firm (14:4).

[Organization] theory focuses on a set of problems that are different from those of the economic theory of the firm. Its problems are not specifically economic; virtually nothing is said about how output levels are set, advertising expenditures determined and so forth. . . . Unlike the theory of the firm, there is not consideration of "aggregation." Indeed, there is nothing to aggregate (7:18).

In fact, then, one of the concepts or variables in economic theory is the firm, or organization. Actions in the market place taken by different firms explain or predict factor prices. In organization theory, the firm (or the organization) is dissected into variables and an attempt is made to explain or predict the behavior of the organization or its members. In short, economic theory tends to look from the firm's boundaries outward, while organization theory looks from the boundaries inward.

Other theories and organization theory. There are other types of theory which have been used in the analysis and investigation of behavior and phenomena which occur in organizations. These may deal with human characteristics and processes such as learning, personality, decision-making, and role. They contain constructs which are an aid in explaining processes or conditions which occur inside, as well as outside, the boundaries of the commonly conceived "organization."

Yet it is important to note that these formulations can serve as the major mechanism or model from which theory about organization can be developed. For instance, learning theory can be used to explain the development of the "expectations" of the members of the organization (33). Much of the "conflict" in the Thompson formulation can be explained in terms of role ambiguity and role conflict, elements of role theory (35). But role theory and learning theory are not organization theory. Though they can be valuable aids in the construction and development of organization theories.

2 An Overview of the Field

● In a much-cited article treating the general subject of organization theory, William Scott defines three major approaches to the theory of organization and outlines the major underpinnings of each. The classical school is described as placing primary emphasis on division of labor, scalar and functional processes, structure, and span of control. The neoclassical school superimposes on these "pillars of classical doctrine...modifications resulting from individual behavior, and the influence of the informal group." Modern organizational theory, relying on empirical research goes beyond both classical and neoclassical. It directs itself toward a system perspective.

In the following selection, Scott deals in detail with these various approaches to conceptualizing organizations, and he presents some interesting and important insights into where organization theory is heading.—H.L.T.

Organization Theory

WILLIAM G. SCOTT

Man is intent on drawing himself into a web of collectivized patterns. "Modern man has learned to accommodate himself to a world increasingly organized. The trend toward every more explicit and consciously drawn relationships is profound and sweeping; it is marked by depth no less than by extension."[1] This comment by Seidenberg nicely summarizes the pervasive influence of organization in many forms of human activity.

Some of the reasons for intense organizational activity are found in the fundamental transitions which revolutionize our society, changing it from a rural culture, to a culture based on technology, industry, and the city. From these changes, a way of life emerged characterized by the *proximity* and *dependency* of people on each other. Proximity and dependency, as

Reprinted by permission of the author and the publisher from the *Journal of the Academy of Management,* vol. 4, no. 1 (April, 1961), pp. 7-26.

conditions of social life, harbor the threats of human conflict, capricious antisocial behavior, instability of human relationships, and uncertainty about the nature of the social structure with its concomitant roles.

Of course, these threats to social integrity are present to some degree in all societies, ranging from the primitive to the modern. But, these threats become dangerous when the harmonious functioning of a society rests on the maintenance of a highly intricate, delicately balanced form of human collaboration. The civilization we have created depends on the preservation of a precarious balance. Hence, disrupting forces impinging on this shaky form of collaboration must be eliminated or minimized.

Traditionally, organization is viewed as a vehicle for accomplishing goals and objectives. While this approach is useful, it tends to obscure the inner workings and internal purposes of organization itself. Another fruitful way of treating organization is as a mechanism having the ultimate purpose of offsetting those forces which undermine human collaboration. In this sense, organization tends to minimize conflict, and to lessen the significance of individual behavior which deviates from values that the organization has established as worthwhile. Further, organization increases stability in human relationships by reducing uncertainty regarding the nature of the system's structure and the human roles which are inherent to it. Corollary to this point, organization enhances the predictability of human action, because it limits the number of behavioral alternatives available to an individual. As Presthus points out:

> Organization is defined as a system of structural interpersonal rela-
> tions . . . individuals are differentiated in terms of authority, status,
> and role with the results that personal interaction is prescribed . . .
>   Anticipated reactions tend to occur, while ambiguity and spontaneity
> are decreased.[2]

In addition to all of this, organization has built-in safeguards. Besides prescribing acceptable forms of behavior for those who elect to submit to it, organization is also able to counterbalance the influence of human action which transcends its established patterns.[3]

Few segments of society have engaged in organizing more intensively than business.[4] The reason is clear. Business depends on what organization offers. Business needs a system of relationships among functions; it needs stability, continuity, and predictability in its internal activities and external contacts. Business also appears to need harmonious relationships among the people and processes which make it up. Put another way, a business organization has to be free, relatively, from destructive tendencies which may be caused by divergent interests.

As a foundation for meeting these needs rests administrative science. A major element of this science is organization theory, which provides the grounds for management activities in a number of significant areas of business endeavor. Organization theory, however, is not a homogeneous science based on generally accepted principles. Various theories of organization have been, and are being evolved. For example, something called "modern organization theory" has recently emerged, raising the wrath of some traditionalists, but also capturing the imagination of a rather elite *avant-garde.*

The thesis of this paper is that modern organization theory, when stripped of its irrelevancies, redundancies, and "speech defects," is a logical and vital evolution in management thought. In order for this thesis to be supported, the reader must endure a review and appraisal of more traditional forms of organization theory which may seem elementary to him.

In any event, three theories of organization are having considerable influence on management thought and practice. They are arbitrarily labeled in this paper as the classical, the neoclassical, and the modern. Each of these is fairly distinct; but they are not unrelated. Also, these theories are on-going, being actively supported by several schools of management thought.

The classical doctrine

For lack of a better method of identification, it will be said that the classical doctrine deals almost exclusively with the *anatomy of formal organization*. This doctrine can be traced back to Frederick W. Taylor's interest in functional foremanship and planning staffs. But most students of management thought would agree that in the United States, the first systematic approach to organization, and the first comprehensive attempt to find organizational universals, is dated 1931 when Mooney and Reiley published *Onward Industry*.[5] Subsequently, numerous books, following the classical vein, have appeared. Two of the more recent are Brech's *Organization*[6] and Allen's *Management and Organization*.[7]

Classical organization theory is built around four key pillars. They are the division of labor, the scalar and functional processes, structure, and span of control. Given these major elements just about all of classical organization theory can be derived.

1) *The division of labor* is without doubt the cornerstone among the four elements.[8] From it the other elements flow as corollaries. For example, *scalar* and *functional* growth requires specialization and departmentalization of functions. Organization *structure* is naturally dependent upon the direction which specialization of activities travels in company development. Finally, *span of control* problems result from the number of specialized functions under the jurisdiction of a manager.

2) *The scalar and functional processes* deal with the vertical and horizontal growth of the organization, respectively.[9] The scalar process refers to the growth of the chain of command, the delegation of authority and responsibility, unity of command, and the obligation to report.

The division of the organization into specialized parts and the regrouping of the parts into compatible units are matters pertaining to the functional process. This process focuses on the horizontal evolution of the line and staff in a formal organization.

3) *Structure* is the logical relationships of functions in an organization, arranged to accomplish the objectives of the company efficiently. Structure implies system and pattern. Classical organization theory usually works with two basic structures, the line and the staff. However, such activities as committee and liaison functions fall quite readily into the purview of

structural considerations. Again, structure is the vehicle for introducing logical and consistent relationships among the diverse functions which comprise the organization.[10]

4) *The span of control* concept relates to the number of subordinates a manager can effectively supervise. Graicunas has been credited with first elaborating the point that there are numerical limitations to the subordinates one man can contro.[11] In a. . . statement on the subject, Brech points out, "span" refers to ". . .the number of persons, themselves carrying managerial and supervisory responsibilities, for whom the senior manager retains his overembracing responsibility of direction and planning co-ordination, motivation, and control."[12] Regardless of interpretation, span of control has significance, in part, for the shape of the organization which evolves through growth. Wide span yields a flat structure; short span results in a tall structure. Further, the span concept directs attention to the complexity of human and functional interrelationships in an organization.

It would not be fair to say that the classical school is unaware of the day-to-day administrative problems of the organization. Paramount among these problems are those stemming from human interactions. But the interplay of individual personality, informal groups, interorganizational conflict, and the decision-making processes in the formal structure appears largely to be neglected by classical organization theory. Additionally, the classical theory overlooks the contributions of the behavioral sciences by failing to incorporate them in its doctrine in any systematic way. In summary, classical organization theory has relevant insights into the nature of organization, but the value of this theory is limited by its narrow concentration on the formal anatomy of organization.

Neoclassical theory of organization

The neoclassical theory of organization embarked on the task of compensating for some of the deficiencies in classical doctrine. The neoclassical school is commonly identified with the human relations movement. Generally, the neoclassical approach takes the postulates of the classical school, regarding the pillars of organization as givens. But these postulates are regarded as modified by people, acting independently or within the context of the informal organization.

One of the main contributions of the neoclassical school is the introduction of behavioral sciences in an integrated fashion into the theory of organization. Through the use of these sciences, the human relationists demonstrate how the pillars of the classical doctrine are affected by the impact of human actions. Further, the neoclassical approach includes a systematic treatment of the informal organization, showing its influence on the formal structure.

Thus, the neoclassical approach to organization theory gives evidence of accepting classical doctrine, but superimposing on it modifications resulting from individual behavior, and the influence of the informal group. The inspiration of the neoclassical school were the Hawthorne studies.[13] Current examples of the neoclassical approach are found in human relations books like Gardner and Moore, *Human Relations in Industry*,[14] and Davis,

Human Relations in Business.[15] To a more limited extent, work in industrial sociology also reflects a neoclassical point of view.[16]

It would be useful to look briefly at some of the contributions made to organization theory by the neoclassicists. First to be considered are modifications of the pillars of classical doctrine; second is the informal organization.

Examples of the neoclassical approach to the pillars of formal organization theory. 1) The *division of labor* has been a long standing subject of comment in the field of human relations. Very early in the history of industrial psychology study was made of industrial fatigue and monotony caused by the specialization of the work.[17] Later, attention shifted to the isolation of the worker, and his feeling of anonymity resulting from insignificant jobs which contributed negligibly to the final product.[18]

Also, specialization influences the work of management. As an organization expands, the need concomitantly arises for managerial motivation and coordination of the activities of others. Both motivation and coordination in turn relate to executive leadership. Thus, in part, stemming from the growth of industrial specialization, the neoclassical school has developed a large body of theory relating to motivation, coordination, and leadership. Much of this theory is derived from the social sciences.

2) Two aspects of the *scalar and functional* processes which have been treated with some degree of intensity by the neoclassical school are the delegation of authority and responsibility, and gaps in or overlapping of functional jurisdictions. The classical theory assumes something of perfection in the delegation and functionalization processes. The neoclassical school points out that human problems are caused by imperfections in the way these processes are handled.

For example, too much or insufficient delegation may render an executive incapable of action. The failure to delegate authority and responsibility equally may result in frustration for the delegatee. Overlapping of authorities often causes clashes in personality. Gaps in authority cause failures in getting jobs done, with one party blaming the other for shortcomings in performance.[19]

The neoclassical school says that the scalar and functional processes are theoretically valid, but tend to deteriorate in practice. The ways in which they break down are described, and some of the human causes are pointed out. In addition the neoclassicists make recommendations, suggesting various "human tools" which will facilitate the operation of these processes.

3) *Structure* provides endless avenues of analysis for the neoclassical theory of organization. The theme is that human behavior disrupts the best laid organizational plans, and thwarts the cleanness of the logical relationships founded in the structure. The neoclassical critique of structure centers on frictions which appear internally among people performing different functions.

Line and staff relations is a problem area, much discussed, in this respect. Many companies seem to have difficulty keeping the line and staff working together harmoniously. Both Dalton[20] and Juran[21] have engaged in research to discover the causes of friction, and to suggest remedies.

Of course, line-staff represent only one of the many problems of structural frictions described by the neoclassicists. As often as not, the neoclassicists will offer prescriptions for the elimination of conflict in structure. Among the more important harmony-rendering formulae are participation, junior boards, bottom-up management, joint committees, recognition of human dignity, and "better" communication.

4) An executive's *span of control* is a function of human determinants, and the reduction of span to a precise, universally applicable ratio is silly, according to the neoclassicists. Some of the determinants of span are individual differences in managerial abilities, the type of people and functions supervised, and the extent of communication effectiveness.

Coupled with the span of control question are the human implications of the type of structure which emerges. That is, is a tall structure with a short span or a flat structure with a wide span more conducive to good human relations than high morale? The answer is situational. Short span results in tight supervision; wide span requires a good deal of delegation with looser controls. Because of individual and organizational differences, sometimes one is better than the other. There is a tendency to favor the looser form of organization, however, for the reason that tall structures breed autocratic leadership, which is often pointed out as a cause of low morale.[22]

The neoclassical view of the informal organization. Nothing more than the barest mention of the informal organization is given even in the most recent classical treatises on organization theory.[23] Systematic discussion of this form of organization has been left to the neoclassicists. The informal organization refers to people in group associations at work, but these associations are not specified in the "blueprint" of the formal organization. The informal organization means natural groupings of people in the work situation.

In a general way, the informal organization appears in response to the social need—the need of people to associate with others. However, for analytical purposes, this explanation is not particularly satisfying. Research has produced the following, more specific determinants underlying the appearance of informal organizations:

1) The *location* determinant simply states that in order to form into groups of any lasting nature, people have to have frequent face-to-face contact. Thus, the geography of physical location in a plant or office is an important factor in predicting who will be in what group.[24]

2) *Occupation* is a key factor determining the rise and composition of informal groups. There is a tendency for people performing similar jobs to group together.[25]

3) *Interests* are another determinant for informal group formation. Even though people might be in the same location, performing similar jobs, differences of interest among them explain why several small, instead of one large, informal organizations emerge.

4) *Special issues* often result in the formation of informal groups, but this determinant is set apart from the three previously mentioned. In this case, people who do not necessarily have similar interests, occupations, or locations may join together for a common cause. Once the issue is resolved, then the tendency is to revert to the more "natural" group forms.[26] Thus,

special issues give rise to a rather impermanent informal association; groups based on the other three determinants tend to be more lasting.

When informal organizations come into being they assume certain characteristics. Since understanding these characteristics is important for management practice, they are noted below:

1) Informal organizations act as agencies of *social control.* They generate a culture based on certain norms of conduct which, in turn, demands conformity from group members. These standards may be at odds with the values set by the formal organization. So an individual may very well find himself in a situation of conflicting demands.

2) The form of human interrelationships in the formal organization requires *techniques of analysis* different from those used to plot the relationships of people in a formal organization. The method used for determining the structure of the informal group is called sociometric analysis. Sociometry reveals the complex structure of interpersonal relations which is based on premises fundamentally unlike the logic of the formal organization.

3) Informal organizations have *status and communication* systems peculiar to themselves, not necessarily derived from the formal systems. For example, the grapevine is the subject of much neoclassical study.

4) Survival of the informal organization requires stable continuing relationships among the people in them. Thus, it has been observed that the informal organization *resists change.*[27] Considerable attention is given by the neoclassicists to overcoming informal resistance to change.

5) The last aspect of analysis which appears to be central to the neoclassical view of the informal organization is the study of the *informal leader.* Discussion revolves around who the informal leader is, how he assumes this role, what characteristics are peculiar to him, and how he can help the manager accomplish his objectives in the formal organization.[28]

This brief sketch of some of the major facets of informal organization theory has neglected, so far, one important topic treated by the neoclassical school. It is the way in which the formal and informal organizations interact.

A conventional way of looking at the interaction of the two is the "live and let live" point of view. Management should recognize that the informal organization exists, nothing can destroy it, and so the executive might just as well work with it. Working with the informal organization involves not threatening its existence unnecessarily, listening to opinions expressed for the group by the leader, allowing group participation in decision-making situations, and controlling the grapevine by prompt release of accurate information.[29]

While this approach is management centered, it is not unreasonable to expect that informal group standards and norms could make themselves felt on formal organizational policy. An honestly conceived effort by managers to establish a working relationship with the informal organization could result in an association where both formal and informal views would be reciprocally modified. The danger which at all costs should be avoided is that "working with the informal organization" does not degenerate into a shallow disguise for human manipulation.

Some neoclassical writing in organization theory, especially that coming from the management-oriented segment of this school, gives the impression that the formal and informal organizations are distinct, and at times, quite irreconcilable factors in a company. The interaction which takes place between the two is something akin to the interaction between the company and a labor union, or a government agency, or another company.

The concept of the social system is another approach to the interactional climate. While this concept can be properly classified as neoclassical, it borders on the modern theories of organization. The phrase "social system" means that an organization is a complex of mutually interdependent, but variable, factors.

These factors include individuals and their attitudes and motives, jobs, the physical work setting, the formal organization, and the informal organizations. These factors, and many others, are woven into an overall pattern of interdependency. From this point of view, the formal and informal organizations lose their distinctiveness, but find real meaning, in terms of human behavior, in the operation of the system as a whole. Thus, the study of organization turns away from descriptions of its component parts, and is refocused on the system of interrelationships among the parts.

One of the major contributions of the Hawthorne studies was the integration of Pareto's idea of the social system into a meaningful method of analysis for the study of behavior in human organizations.[30] This concept is still vitally important. But unfortunately some work in the field of human relations undertaken by the neoclassicists has overlooked, or perhaps discounted, the significance of this consideration.[31]

The fundamental insight regarding the social system, developed and applied to the industrial scene by the Hawthorne researchers, did not find much extension in subsequent work in the neoclassical vein. Indeed, the neoclassical school after the Hawthorne studies generally seemed content to engage in descriptive generalizations, or particularized empirical research studies which did not have much meaning outside their own context.

The neoclassical school of organization theory has been called bankrupt. Criticisms range from, "human relations is a tool for cynical puppeteering of people," to "human relations is nothing more than a trifling body of empirical and descriptive information." There is a good deal of truth in both criticisms, but another appraisal of the neoclassical school of organization theory is offered here. The neoclassical approach has provided valuable contributions to lore of organization. But, like the classical theory, the neoclassical doctrine suffers from incompleteness, a shortsighted perspective, and lack of integration among the many facets of human behavior studied by it. Modern organization theory has made a move to cover the shortcomings of the current body of theoretical knowledge.

Modern organization theory

The distinctive qualities of modern organization theory are its conceptual-analytical base, its reliance on empirical research data and, above all, its integrating nature. These qualities are framed in a philosophy which accepts the premise that the only meaningful way to study organization is to study it as a system. As Henderson put it, the study of a system must rely on a method of analysis, ". . .involving the simultaneous variations of mutually dependent variables."[32] Human systems, of course, contain a huge number of dependent variables which defy the most complex simultaneous equations to solve.

Nevertheless, system analysis has its own peculiar point of view which aims to study organization in the way Henderson suggests. It treats organization as a system of mutually dependent variables. As a result, modern organization theory, which accepts system analysis, shifts the conceptual level of organization study above the classical and neoclassical theories. Modern organization theory asks a range of interrelated questions which are not seriously considered by the two other theories.

Key among these questions are: (1) What are the strategic parts of the system? (2) What is the nature of their mutual dependency? (3) What are the main processes in the system which link the parts together, and facilitate their adjustments to each other? (4) What are the goals sought by systems?[33]

Modern organization theory is in no way a unified body of thought. Each writer and researcher has his special emphasis when he considers the system. Perhaps the most evident unifying thread in the study of systems is the effort to look at the organization in its totality. Representative books in this field are March and Simon, *Organizations,*[34] and Haire's anthology, *Modern Organization Theory.*[35]

Instead of attempting a review of different writers' contributions to modern organization theory, it will be more useful to discuss the various ingredients involved in system analysis. They are the parts, the interactions, the processes, and the goals of systems.

The parts of the system and their interdependency. The first basic part of the system is the *individual,* and the personality structure he brings to the organization. Elementary to an individual's personality are motives and attitudes which condition the range of expectancies he hopes to satisfy by participating in the system.

The second part of the system is the formal arrangement of functions, usually called the *formal organization.* The formal organization is the interrelated pattern of jobs which make up the structure of a system. Certain writers, like Argyris, see a fundamental conflict resulting from the demands made by the system, and the structure of the mature, normal personality. In any event, the individual has expectancies regarding the job he is to perform; and conversely, the job makes demands on, or has expectancies relating to, the performance of the individual. Considerable attention has been given by writers in modern organization theory to incongruencies resulting from the interaction of organizational and individual demands.[36]

The third part in the organization system is the *informal organization.* Enough has been said already about the nature of this organization. But it must be noted that an interactional pattern exists between the individual and the informal group. This interactional arrangement can be conveniently discussed as the mutual modification of expectancies. The informal organization has demands which it makes on members in terms of anticipated forms of behavior and the individual has expectancies of satisfaction he hopes to derive from association with people on the job. Both these sets of expectancies interact, resulting in the individual modifying his behavior to accord with the demands of the group, and the group, perhaps, modifying what it expects from an individual because of the impact of his personality on group norms.[37]

Much of what has been said about the various expectancy systems in an organization can also be treated using status and role concepts. Part of modern organization theory rests on research findings in social-psychology relative to reciprocal patterns of behavior stemming from role demands generated by both the formal and informal organizations, and role perceptions peculiar to the individual. Bakke's *fusion process* is largely concerned with the modification of role expectancies. The fusion process is a force, according to Bakke, which acts to weld divergent elements together for the preservation of organizational integrity.[38]

The fifth part of system analysis is the *physical setting* in which the job is performed. Although this element of the system may be implicit in what has been said already about the formal organization and its functions, it is well to separate it. In the physical surroundings of work, interactions are present in complex man-machine systems. The human "engineer" cannot approach the problems posed by such interrelationships in a purely technical, engineering fashion. As Haire says, these problems lie in the domain of the social theorist.[39] Attention must be centered on responses demanded from a logically ordered production function, often with the view of minimizing the error in the system. From this standpoint, work cannot be effectively organized unless the psychological, social, and physiological characteristics of people participating in the work environment are considered. Machines and processes should be designed to fit certain generally observed psychological and physiological properties of men, rather than hiring men to fit machines.

In summary, the parts of the system which appear to be of strategic importance are the individual, the formal structure, the informal organization, status and role patterns, and the physical environment of work. Again, these parts are woven into a configuration called the organizational system. The processes which link the parts are taken up next.

The linking process. One can say, with a good deal of glibness, that all the parts mentioned above are interrelated. Although this observation is quite correct, it does not mean too much in terms of system theory unless some attempt is made to analyze the processes by which the interaction is achieved. Role theory is devoted to certain types of interactional processes. In addition, modern organization theorists point to three other linking activities which appear to be universal to human systems of organized behavior. These processes are communication, balance, and decision making.

1) Communication is mentioned often in neoclassical theory, but the emphasis is on description of forms of communication activity, i.e., formal-informal, vertical-horizontal, line-staff. Communication, as a

mechanism which links the segments of the system together, is overlooked by way of much considered analysis.

One aspect of modern organization theory is study of the communication network in the system. Communication is viewed as the method by which action is evoked from the parts of the system. Communication acts not only as stimuli resulting in action, but also as a control and coordination mechanism linking the decision centers in the system into a synchronized pattern. Deutsch points out that organizations are composed of parts which communicate with each other, receive messages from the outside world, and store information. Taken together, these communication functions of the parts comprise a configuration representing the total system.[40] More is to be said about communication later in the discussion of the cybernetic model.

2) The concept of *balance* as a linking process involves a series of some rather complex ideas. Balance refers to an equilibrating mechanism whereby the various parts of the system are maintained in a harmoniously structured relationship to each other.

The necessity for the balance concept logically flows from the nature of systems themselves. It is impossible to conceive of an ordered relationship among the parts of a system without also introducing the idea of a stabilizing or an adapting mechanism.

Balance appears in two varieties—quasi-automatic and innovative. Both forms of balance act to insure system integrity in face of changing conditions, either internal or external to the system. The first form of balance, quasi-automatic, refers to what some think are "homeostatic" properties of systems. That is, systems seem to exhibit built-in propensities to maintain steady states.

If human organizations are open, self-maintaining systems, then control and regulatory processes are necessary. The issue hinges on the degree to which stabilizing processes in systems, when adapting to change, are automatic. March and Simon have an interesting answer to this problem, which in part is based on the type of change and the adjustment necessary to adapt to the change. Systems have programs of action which are put into effect when a change is perceived. If the change is relatively minor, and if the change comes within the purview of established programs of action, then it might be fairly confidently predicted that the adaptation made by the system will be quasi-automatic.[41]

The role of innovative, creative balancing efforts now needs to be examined. The need for innovation arises when adaptation to a change is outside the scope of existing programs designed for the purpose of keeping the system in balance. New programs have to be evolved in order for the system to maintain internal harmony.

New programs are created by trial and error search for feasible action alternatives to cope with a given change. But innovation is subject to the limitations and possibilities inherent in the quantity and variety of information present in a system at a particular time. New combinations of alternatives for innovative purposes depend on:

1) The possible range of output of the system, or the capacity of the system to supply information.

2) The range of available information in the memory of the system.

3) The operating rules (program) governing the analysis and flow of information within the system.

4) The ability of the system to "forget" previously learned solutions to change problems.[42] A system with too good a memory might narrow its behavioral choices to such an extent as to stifle innovation. In simpler language, old learning programs might be used to adapt to the change, when newly innovated programs are necessary.[43]

Much of what has been said about communication and balance brings to mind a cybernetic model in which both these processes have vital roles. Cybernetics has to do with feedback and control of all kinds of systems. Its purpose is to maintain system stability in the face of change. Cybernetics cannot be studied without considering communication networks, information flow, and some kind of balancing process aimed at preserving the integrity of the system.

Cybernetics direct attention to key questions regarding the system. These questions are: how are communication centers connected, and how are they maintained? Corollary to this question: what is the structure of the feedback system? Next, what information is stored in the organization, and at what points? And as a corollary: how accessible is this information to decision-making centers? Third, how conscious is the organization of the operation of its own parts? That is, to what extent do the policy centers receive control information with sufficient frequency and relevancy to create a real awareness of the operation of the segments of the system? Finally, what are the learning (innovating) capabilities of the system?[44]

Answers to the questions posed by cybernetics are crucial to understanding both the balancing and communication processes in systems.[45] Although cybernetics has been applied largely to technical-engineering problems of automation, the model of feedback, control, and regulation in all systems has a good deal of generality. Cybernetics is a fruitful area which can be used to synthesize the processes of communication and balance.

3) A wide spectrum of topics dealing with types of decisions in human systems makes up the core of analysis of another important process in organizations. Decision analysis is one of the major contributions of March and Simon in their book *Organizations*. The two major classes of decisions they discuss are decisions to produce and decisions to participate in the system.[46]

Decisions to produce are largely a result of an interaction between individual attitudes and the demands of organization. Motivation analysis becomes central to studying the nature and results of the interaction. Individual decisions to participate in the organization reflect on such issues as the relationship between organizational rewards versus the demands made by the organization. Participation decisions also focus attention on the reasons why individuals remain in or leave organizations.

March and Simon treat decisions as internal variables in an organization which depend on jobs, individual expectations and motivations, and organizational structure. Marschak[47] looks on the decision process as an independent variable upon which the survival of the organization is based. In this case, the organization is reviewed as having, inherent in its structure, the ability to maximize survival requisites through its established decision process.

The goals of organization. Organization has three goals which may be either intermeshed or independent ends in themselves. They are growth, stability, and interaction. The last goal refers to organizations which exist primarily to provide a medium for association of its members with others. Interestingly enough these goals seem to apply to different forms of organization at varying levels of complexity, ranging from simple clockwork mechanisms to social systems.

These similarities in organizational purposes have been observed by a number of people, and a field of thought and research called system theory has developed, dedicated to the task of discovering organizational universals. The dream of general system theory is to create a science of organizational universals, or if you will, a universal science using common organizational elements found in all systems as a starting point.

Modern organization theory is on the periphery of general system theory. Both general system theory and modern organization theory studies:

1) The parts (individuals) in aggregates, and the movement of individuals into and out of the system.

2) The interaction of individuals with the environment found in the system.

3) The interactions among individuals in the system.

4) General growth and stability problems of systems.[48]

Modern organization theory and general system theory are similar in that they look at organization as an integrated whole. They differ, however, in terms of their generality. General system theory is concerned with every level of system, whereas modern organizational theory focuses primarily on human organization.

The question might be asked, what can the science of administration gain by the study of system levels other than human? Before attempting an answer, note should be made of what these other levels are. Boulding presents a convenient method of classification:

1) The static structure—a level of framework, the anatomy of a system; for example, the structure of the universe.

2) The simple dynamics system—the level of clockworks, predetermined necessary motions.

3) The cybernetic system—the level of the thermostat, the system moves to maintain a given equilibrium through a process of self-regulation.

4) The open system—level of self-maintaining systems, moves toward and includes living organisms.

5) The genetic-societal system—level of cell society, characterized by a division of labor among cells.

6) Animal systems—level of mobility, evidence of goal-directed behavior.

7) Human systems—level of symbol interpretation and idea communication.

8) Social system—level of human organization.

9) Transcendental systems—level of ultimates and absolutes which exhibit systematic structure but are unknowable in essence.[49]

This approach to the study of systems by finding universals common at all levels of organization offers intriguing possibilities for administrative organization theory. A good deal of light could be thrown on social systems if structurally analogous elements could be found in the simpler types of systems. For example, cybernetic systems have characteristics which seem to be similar to feedback, regulation, and control phenomena in human organizations. Thus, certain facets of cybernetic models could be generalized to human organization. Considerable danger, however, lies in poorly founded analogies. Superficial similarities between simpler system forms and social systems are apparent everywhere. Instinctually based ant societies, for example, do not yield particularly instructive lessons for understanding rationally conceived human organizations. Thus, care should be taken that analogies used to bridge system levels are not mere devices for literary enrichment. For analogies to have usefulness and validity, they must exhibit inherent structural similarities or implicity identical operational principles.[50]

Modern organization theory leads, as it has been shown, almost inevitably into a discussion of general system theory. A science of organizational universals has some strong advocates, particularly among biologists.[51] Organization theorists in administrative science cannot afford to overlook the contributions of general system theory. Indeed, modern organization concepts could offer a great deal to those working with general system theory. But the ideas dealt with in the general theory are exceedingly elusive.

Speaking of the concept of equilibrium as a unifying element in all systems, Easton says, "It (equilibrium) leaves the impression that we have a useful general theory when in fact, lacking measurability, it is a mere pretense for knowledge."[52] The inability to quantify and measure universal organization elements undermines the success of pragmatic tests to which general system theory might be put.

Organization theory: Quo vadis? Most sciences have a vision of the universe to which they are applied, and administrative science is not an exception. This universe is composed of parts. One purpose of science is to synthesize the parts into an organized conception of its field of study. As a science matures, its theorems about the configuration of its universe change. The direction of change in three sciences, physics, economics, and sociology, are noted briefly for comparison with the development of an administrative view of human organization.

The first comprehensive and empirically verifiable outlook of the physical universe was presented by Newton in his *Principia*. Classical physics, founded on Newton's work, constitutes a grand scheme in which a wide range of physical phenomena could be organized and predicted. Newtonian physics may rightfully be regarded as the "macro" in nature, because its system of organization was concerned largely with gross events of which the movement of celestial bodies, waves, energy forms, and strain are examples. For years classical physics was supreme, being applied continuously to smaller and smaller classes of phenomena in the physical universe. Physicists at one time adopted the view that everything in their realm could be covered by simply subdividing problems. Physics thus moved into the "micro" order.

But in the nineteenth century a revolution took place motivated largely because events were being noted which could not be explained adequately by the conceptual framework supplied by the classical school. The consequences of this revolution are brilliantly described by Eddington:

> From the point of view of philosophy of science the conception associated with entropy must I think be ranked as the great contribution of the nineteenth century to scientific thought. It marked a reaction from the view that everything to which science need pay attention is discovered by microscopic dissection of objects. It provided an alternative standpoint in which the centre of interest is shifted from the entities reached by the customary analysis (atoms, electric potentials, etc.) to qualities possessed by the system as a whole, which cannot be split up and located—a little bit here, and a little bit there. . . .
>
> We often think that when we have completed our study of *one* we know all about *two* because "two" is "one and one." We forget that we have still to make a study of "and." Secondary physics is the study of "and"—that is to say, of organization.[53]

Although modern physics often deals in minute quantities and oscillations, the conception of the physicist is on the "macro" scale. He is concerned with the "and," or the organization of the world in which the event occur. These developments did not invalidate classical physics as to its usefulness for explaining a certain range of phenomena. But classical physics is no longer the undisputed law of the universe. It is a special case.

Early economic theory, and Adam Smith's *Wealth of Nations* comes to mind, examined economic problems in the macro order. The *Wealth of Nations* is mainly concerned with matters of national income and welfare. Later, the economics of the firm, micro-economics, dominated the theoretical scene in this science. And, finally, with Keynes' *The General Theory of Employment Interest and Money*, a systematic approach to the economic universe was reintroduced on the macro level.

The first era of the developing science of sociology was occupied by the great social "system builders." Comte, the so-called father of sociology, had a macro view of society in that his chief works are devoted to social reorganization. Comte was concerned with the interrelationships among social, political, religious, and educational institutions. As sociology progressed, the science of society compressed. Emphasis shifted from the macro approach of the pioneers to the detailed, empirical study of small social units. The compression of sociological analysis was accompanied by study of social pathology or disorganization.

In general, physics, economics, and sociology appear to have two things in common. First, they offered a macro point of view as their initial systematic comprehension of their area of study. Second, as the science developed, attention fragmented into analysis of the parts of the organization, rather than attending to the system as a whole. This is the micro phase.

In physics and economics, discontent was evidenced by some scientists at the continual atomization of the universe. The reaction to the micro approach was a new theory or theories dealing with the total system, on the macro level again. This third phase of scientific development seems to be more evident in physics and economics than sociology.

The reason for the "macro-micro-macro" order of scientific progress lies, perhaps, in the hypothesis that usually the things which strike man first are of great magnitude. The scientist attempts to discover order in the vastness. But after macro laws or models of systems are postulated, variations appear which demand analysis, not so much in terms of the entire system, but more in terms of the specific parts which make it up. Then, intense study of microcosm may result in new general laws, replacing the old models of organization. Or, the old and the new models may stand together, each explaining a different class of phenomenon. Or, the old and the new concepts of organization may be welded to produce a single creative synthesis.

Now, what does all this have to do with the problem of organization in administrative science? Organization concepts seem to have gone through the same order of development in this field as in the three just mentioned. It is evident that the classical theory of organization, particularly as in the work of Mooney and Reiley, is concerned with principles common to all organizations. It is a macro-organization view. The classical approach to organization, however, dealt with the gross anatomical parts and processes of the formal organization. Like classical physics, the classical theory of organization is a special case. Neither are especially well equipped to account for variation from their established framework.

Many variations in the classical administrative model result from human behavior. The only way these variations could be understood was by a microscopic examination of particularized, situational aspects of human behavior. The mission of the neoclassical school thus is "micro-analysis."

It was observed earlier, that somewhere along the line the concept of the social system, which is the key to understanding the Hawthorne studies, faded into the background. Maybe the idea is so obvious that it was lost to the view of researchers and writers in human relations. In any event, the press of research in the microcosmic universes of the informal organization, morale and productivity leadership, participation, and the like forced the notion of the social system into limbo. Now, with the advent of modern organization theory, the social system has been resurrected.

Modern organization theory appears to be concerned with Eddington's "and." This school claims that its operational hypothesis is based on a macro point of view; that is, the study of organization as a whole. This nobility of purpose should not obscure, however, certain difficulties faced by this field as it is presently constituted. Modern organization theory raises two questions which should be explored further. First, would it not be more accurate to speak of modern organization theor*ies*? Second, just how much of modern organization theory is modern?

The first question can be answered with a quick affirmative. Aside from the notion of the system, there are few, if any, other ideas of a unifying nature. Except for several important exceptions,[54] modern organization theorists tend to pursue their pet points of view,[55] suggesting they are part of system theory, but not troubling to show by what mystical means they arrive at this conclusion.

The irony of it all is that a field dealing with systems has, indeed, little system. Modern organization theory needs a framework, and it needs an integration of issues into a common conception of organization. Admittedly, this is a large order. But it is curious not to find serious analytical treatment of subjects like cybernetics or general system theory in Haire's *Modern Organizational Theory*, which claims to be a representative example of work in this field. Beer has ample evidence in his book *Cybernetics and Management* that cybernetics, if imaginatively approached, provides a valuable conceptual base for the study of systems.

The second question suggests an ambiguous answer. Modern organization theory is in part a product of the past; system analysis is not a new idea. Further, modern organization theory relies for supporting data on microcosmic research studies, generally drawn from the journals of the last ten years. The newness of modern organization theory, perhaps, is its effort to snythesize recent research contributions of many fields into a system theory characterized by a reoriented conception of organization.

One might ask, but what is the modern theorist reorienting? A clue is found in the almost snobbish disdain assumed by some authors of the neoclassical human relations school, and particularly, the classical school. Re-evaluation of the classical school of organization is overdue. However, this does· not mean that its contributions to organization theory are irrelevent and should be overlooked in the rush to get on the "behavioral science bandwagon."

Haire announces that the papers appearing in *Modern Organization Theory* constitute, "the ragged leading edge of a wave of theoretical development." [56] Ragged, yes; but leading no! The papers appearing in this book do not represent a theoretical breakthrough in the concept of organization. Haire's collection is an interesting potpourri with several contributions of considerable significance. But readers should beware that they will not find vastly new insights into organizational behavior in this book, if they have kept up with the literature of the social sciences, and have dabbled to some extent in the esoteria of biological theories of growth, information theory, and mathematical model building. For those who have not maintained the pace, *Modern Organization Theory* serves the admirable purpose of bringing them up-to-date on a rather diversified number of subjects.

Some work in modern organization theory is pioneering, making its appraisal difficult and future uncertain. While the direction of this endeavor is unclear, one thing is patently true. Human behavior in organizations, and indeed, organization itself, cannot be adequately understood within the ground rules of classical and neoclassical doctrines. Appreciation of human organization requires a *creative* synthesis of massive amounts of empirical data, a high order of deductive reasoning, imaginative research studies, and a taste for individual and social values. Accomplishment of all these objectives, and the inclusion of them into a framework of the concept of the system, appears to be the goal of modern organization theory. The vitality of administrative science rests on the advances modern theorists make along this line.

Modern organization theory, 1960 style, is an amorphous aggregation of synthesizers and restaters, with a few extending leadership on the frontier. For the sake of these few, it is well to admonish that pouring old wine into new bottles may make the spirits cloudy. Unfortunately, modern organization theory has almost succeeded in achieving the status of a fad. Popularization and exploitation contributed to the disrepute into which human relations has fallen. It would be a great waste if modern organization theory yields to the same fate, particularly since both modern organization theory and human relations draw from the same promising source of inspiration—system analysis.

Modern organization theory needs tools of analysis and a conceptual framework uniquely its own, but it must also allow for the incorporation of relevant contributions of many fields. It may be that the framework will come from general system theory. New areas of research such as decision theory, information theory, and cybernetics also offer reasonable expectations of analytical and conceptual tools. Modern organization theory represents a frontier of research which has great significance for management. The potential is great, because it offers the opportunity for uniting what is valuable in classical theory with the social and natural sciences into a systematic and integrated conception of human organization.

Footnotes

[1] Roderick Seidenburg, *Post Historic Man* (Boston: Beacon Press, 1951), p. 1.

[2] Robert V. Presthus, "Toward a Theory of Organizational Behavior," *Administrative Science Quarterly* (June, 1958), p. 50.

[3] Regulation and predictability of human behavior are matters of degree varying with different organizations on something of a continuum. At one extreme are bureaucratic type organizations with tight bonds of regulation. At the other extreme are voluntary associations, and informal organizations with relatively loose bonds of regulation.

This point has an interesting sidelight. A bureaucracy with tight controls and a high degree of predictability of human action appears to be unable to distinguish between destructive and creative deviations from established values. Thus the only thing which is safeguarded is the *status quo*.

[4] The monolithic institutions of the military and government are other cases of organizational preoccupation.

[5] James D. Mooney and Alan C. Reiley, *Onward Industry* (New York: Harper and Brothers, 1931). Later published by James D. Mooney under the title *Principles of Organization.*

[6] E.F.L. Brech, *Organization* (London: Longmans, Green and Company, 1957).

[7] Louis A. Allen, *Management and Organization* (New York: McGraw-Hill Book Company, 1958).

[8] Usually the division of labor is treated under a topical heading of departmentation, see for example: Harold Koontz and Cyril O'Donnell, *Principles of Management* (New York: McGraw-Hill Book Company, 1959), chapter 7.

[9] These processes are discussed at length in Ralph Currier Davis, *The Fundamentals of Top Management* (New York: Harper Brothers, 1951), chapter 7.

[10] For a discussion of structure, see William H. Newman, *Administrative Action* (Englewood Cliffs, New Jersey: Prentice-Hall, Incorporated, 1951), chapter 16.

[11] V. A. Graicunas, "Relationships in Organization," *Papers on the Science of Administration* (New York: Columbia University, 1937).

[12] Brech, *op. cit.*, p. 78.

[13] See F. J. Roethlisberger and William J. Dickson, *Management and the Worker* (Cambridge: Harvard University Press, 1939).

[14] Burleigh B. Gardner and David G. Moore, *Human Relations in Industry* (Homewood, Illinois: Richard D. Irwin, 1955).

[15] Keith Davis, *Human Relations in Business* (New York: McGraw-Hill Book Company, 1957).

16 For example, see Delbert C. Miller and William H. Form, *Industrial Sociology* (New York: Harper and Brothers, 1951).

17 See Hugo Munsterberg, *Psychology and Industrial Efficiency* (Boston: Houghton Mifflin Company, 1913).

18 Probably the classic work is Elton Mayo, *The Human Problems of an Industrial Civilization* (Cambridge: Harvard University, 1946, first printed 1933).

19 For further discussion of the human relations implications of the scalar and functional processes, see Keith Davis, *op. cit.,* pp. 60-66.

20 Melville Dalton, "Conflicts Between Staff and Line Managerial Officers," *American Sociological Review* (June, 1950), pp. 342-51.

21 J. M. Juran, "Improving the Relationships Between Staff and Line," *Personnel* (May, 1956), pp. 515-24.

22 Gardner and Moore, *op. cit.,* pp. 237-43.

23 For example, Brech, *op. cit.,* pp. 27-29, and Allen, *op. cit.,* pp. 61-62.

24 See Leon Festinger, Stanley Schachter, and Kurt Back, *Social Pressures in Informal Groups* (New York: Harper and Brothers, 1950), pp. 153-63.

25 For example, see W. Fred Cottrell, *The Railroader* (Palo Alto: The Stanford University Press, 1940), chapter 3.

26 Except in cases where the existence of an organization is necessary for the continued maintenance of employee interest. Under these conditions the previously informal association may emerge as a formal group, such as a union.

27 Probably the classic study of resistance to change is Lester Coch and John R. P. French, Jr., "Overcoming Resistance to Change," in Schuyler Dean Hoslett (editor) *Human Factors in Management* (New York: Harper and Brothers, 1951), pp. 242-68.

28 For example, see Robert Saltonstall, *Human Relations in Administration* (New York: McGraw-Hill Book Company, 1959), pp. 330-31; and Keith Davis, *op. cit.,* pp. 99-101.

29 For an example of this approach, see John T. Doutt, "Management Must Manage the Informal Group, Too," *Advanced Management* (May, 1959), pp. 26-28.

30 See Roethlisberger and Dickson, *op. cit.,* Chapter 24.

31 A check of management human relations texts, the organization and human relations chapters of principles of management texts, and texts on conventional organization theory for management courses reveals little or no treatment of the concept of the social system.

32 Lawrence J. Henderson, *Pareto's General Sociology* (Cambridge: Harvard University Press, 1935), p. 13.

33 There is another question which cannot be treated in the scope of this paper. It asks, what research tools should be used for the study of the system?

34 James G. March and Herbert A. Simon, *Organizations* (New York: John Wiley and Sons, 1958).

35 Mason Haire (editor), *Modern Organization Theory* (New York: John Wiley and Sons, 1959).

36 See Chris Argyris, *Personality and Organization* (New York: Harper and Brothers, 1957), esp. chapters 2, 3, 7.

37 For a larger treatment of this subject, see George C. Homans, *The Human Group* (New York: Harcourt, Brace and Company, 1950), chapter 5.

38 E. Wight Bakke, "Concept of the Social Organization," in *Modern Organization Theory,* Mason Haire (editor) (New York: John Wiley and Sons, 1959), pp. 60-61.

39 Mason Haire, "Psychology and the Study of Business: Joint Behavioral Sciences," in *Social Science Research on Business: Product and Potential* (New York: Columbia University Press, 1959), pp. 53-59.

40 Karl W. Deutsch "On communication Models in the Social Sciences," *Public Opinion Quarterly,* 16 (1952), pp. 356-80.

41 March and Simon, *op. cit.,* pp. 139-40.

42 Mervyn L. Cadwallader "The Cybernetic Analysis of Change in Complex Social Organization," *The American Journal of Sociology* (September, 1959), p. 156.

43 It is conceivable for innovative behavior to be programmed into the system.

44 These are questions adapted from Deutsch, *op. cit.,* 365-70.

45 Answers to these questions would require a comprehensive volume. One of the best approaches currently available is Stafford Beer, *Cybernetics and Management* (New York: John Wiley and Sons, 1959).

46 March and Simon, *op. cit.,* chapters 3 and 4.

47 Jacob Marschak, "Efficient and Viable Organizational Forms" in *Modern Organization Theory*, Mason Haire (editor) (New York: John Wiley and Sons, 1959), pp. 307-20.

48 Kenneth E. Boulding, "General System Theory—The Skeleton of Science," *Management Science* (April, 1956), pp. 200-02.

49 *Ibid.*, pp. 202-05.

50 Seidenberg, *op. cit.*, p. 136. The fruitful use of the type of analogies spoken of by Seidenberg is evident in the application of thermodynamic principles, particularly the entropy concept, to communication theory. See Claude E. Shannon and Warren Weaver, *The Mathematical Theory of Communication* (Urbana: The University of Illinois Press, 1949). Further, the existence of a complete analogy between the operational behavior of thermodynamic systems, electrical communication systems, and biological systems has been noted by Y. S. Touloukian, *The Concept of Entropy in Communication, Living Organisms, and Thermodynamics,* Research Bulletin 130, Purdue Engineering Experiment Station.

51 For example, see Ludwig von Bertalanffy, *Problem of Life* (London: Watts and Company, 1952).

52 David Easton, "Limits of the Equilibrium Model in Social Research," in *Profits and Problems of Homeostatic Models in the Behavioral Sciences.* Publication 1, Chicago Behavioral Sciences (1953), p. 30.

53 Sir Arthur Eddington, *The Nature of the Physical World* (Ann Arbor: The University of Michigan Press, 1958), pp. 103-04.

54 For example, E. Wight Bakke, *op. cit.*, pp. 18-75.

55 There is a large selection including decision theory, individual-organization interaction, motivation, vitality, stability, growth, and graph theory, to mention a few.

56 Mason Haire, "General Issues," in Mason Haire (editor), *Modern Organization Theory* (New York: John Wiley and Sons, 1959), p. 2.

3 Classical Theory

● The classical theorists, as described by Scott, deal extensively with the anatomy of formal organization. The work of Ralph C. Davis is representative of this approach. In it he deals with most of the variables typically associated with this school of thought.

Davis' work falls into the group that Krupp (14) calls "design theory" and James Thompson (34) calls "administrative management," part of the closed system strategy for studying organization. This is a "rational" approach to organization. Once goals of the organization have been determined, or specified, then the development of structure, the flow of authority, and the other relationships clearly follow in a logical fashion. It is, however, important to note that such a strategy does not preclude other important considerations.

Before we delve more deeply into the structure of the theory, let us comment on two of its major aspects, the nature of objectives and the authority/responsibility question.

Davis has as a point of departure the notion that the primary objective of a business organization is an economic service. This is based on the simple question of survival. There is no justification for an economic organization that is not providing economic values. Therefore, to survive, the firm must produce some salable values. These values are created by work and they are the beginning point of the logical development of structure; that is, organization structure needs to be developed in a way that will facilitate providing these values to the consuming public of the organization. Translation of these objectives into products, or services, leads to the determination of activities necessary to create them. These activities are grouped together in such a way as to form the structure of the organization. It does not seem unreasonable to conclude in terms of hierarchy and distribution of authority that the structure of the organization, since it is contingent upon the objectives, depends upon what the objective is.

The second aspect for comment is authority. The notion of authority parallels that of other classical organization theorists. Authority is viewed as a function of, or contingent upon, the position to which one is assigned in the organization and it derives from the duties and obligations attendant to the particular job or assignment.

To achieve the goals of the organization—that is, to provide the values expected by the consumers—certain activities must be performed. Carrying out these activities is the responsibility of the individual in the position. Thus, responsibility is the obligation to perform an assignment which one accepts when he takes a position with an organization. In order to carry out these obligations, the individual must be able to utilize, direct, and allocate both physical and human resources. When these are at his disposal, and this is formally specified, then his "right" to utilize them has been determined. In this situation the person is said to have "authority."

The notion of formal authority, as used in the classical approach, does not seem to be an active, or an action, concept. It does not imply that members will take some action that is prescribed for them or that the holder of these rights to utilize resources will exercise them. It refers only to the organizational right of the incumbent. Another concept is required to activate compliance. Power is the "force which maintains the right." When power is exerted, some action will be taken by the subordinates. This power may be physical, or it may be moral, but it is power, not rights, which activates compliance.

What makes this authority legitimate? Because it has been treated so often in the literature of organization theory, this seems an important question. The basis for the legitimation of authority in the Davis formulation, as well as in those by other classical writers, rests on how it is related to the right of private property. Individuals have rights to utilize their property, within some constraints, as they see fit. The right of the private business organization to use resources depends upon the delegation, to the owners of the business, of the property rights by organized society through its representatives. The right of an executive to plan, organize, and control the use by the business organization is a right delegated by ownership.

Within the organization, of course, the amount of authority and responsibility in any one position is a function largely of the manner and the degree in which the general objectives have been factored into activities and responsibilities for that position. Therefore, the right of a manager (or his authority), at any level in the organization, can be traced back to the property rights of individuals in the society in general.

The concept of authority in the classical theory deals with formal, documented rights. It does not include reasons why individuals comply. Since there is generally only limited treatment of reasons why people comply with demands from authority in the classical theory, a number of criticisms of the theory have emerged. This has led to points of view about authority that are expressed in other theories presented in this book—H.L.T.

Fundamentals of Top Management

RALPH C. DAVIS

Management is the function of executive leadership. Its organic subfunctions are the creative planning, organizing, and controlling of the organizational activities for which the executive is responsible. They have to do with the accomplishment of the group and project objectives of the organization.

Creative planning provides the answers to such questions as what should be done, how and where it should be done, who should do it, what physical and human resources are necessary for the accomplishment of the particular mission, and other questions of a similar nature. Its purpose is to determine an effective, economical basis for the accomplishment of designated objectives.

Organizing sets up the common, basic conditions that underlie effective, economical execution by a particular group over a period of time. They must be created before work starts on the kinds of activities for which they are a prerequisite. These general conditions are specified in the plan, or derived from it.

Controlling constrains and regulates action in accordance with the requirements of the plan. Business standards are criteria that enable us to measure, proportion, and maintain business factors, forces, and effects in proper condition and relation to one another. They are necessary for the satisfactory performance of all management functions. Effective, economical execution requires these conditions and relationships to be adequately standardized.

There must be and is a body of related knowledge that concerns the solution of management problems. The pioneers in the field recognized this fact clearly at the turn of the century. They saw the need for a science of management. The term science seems to perturb some people unnecessarily. It may refer to any classified body of fundamental facts, principles, and techniques that explains certain basic phenomena. It supplies a basis for the solution of problems associated with these phenomena.

Scientific management attempts to apply the logic of effective thinking to the solution of business problems. It depends on and leads to a further development of a philosophy of management. The latter is any system of thought that explains basic business problems. It is based on logical relationships between business factors, forces, effects, and principles. It must supply the basis for an intelligent approach to the solution of these problems. The principal problems have to do with business objectives, standards of business conduct, executive leadership, business policy, business functions, personnel, physical performance factors, organization structure, business procedure, and organization morale.

The consuming public does not exist to serve the owners and employees of business organizations. Business exists to serve the public. The sanctions that enable the owners of business establishments to engage in private enterprise rest on the individual's right of private property in his capital. This right is the basis of free enterprise. The sanctions that enable either executive or operative employees to engage in individual or collective bargaining are based on the individual's right of private property in his services. The right is the basis of free labor. The right of private property is delegated by the body politic through its elected representatives. It can be modified if it is abused by either labor or capital. It has been so abused in the past. Such modifications move in the direction of state capitalism and socialism, even though they may be necessary.

There are certain obligations that are a condition of the granting of the right of private property for the performance of economic functions. They have to do basically with the obligation to provide the public with the goods and services it requires in the quantities and qualities it desires, when and where it wants them and at a competitive price. They require the maintenance of free competition and free markets for both capital and labor, subject to such a minimum of government regulation as may be necessary in the public interest. They require the maintenance of the customer's right of freedom of choice in the market to the maximum degree that is practicable.

An objective is any value or values that are needed or desired by an individual or group, provided that the person or group is willing to make some sacrifice or effort to obtain them. An economic value is any satisfaction of need or a desire for which an individual or group is willing to exchange other values. These values may or may not be tangible. The primary objective of the business organization is necessarily its service objectives. They are customer satisfactions, in terms of business' basic obligation to supply goods and services as required. The desire or need of owners for a profit and of employees for a wage are collateral objectives. They are earned to the extent that the public is well served. The business organization also has certain secondary objectives. They have to do with economy and effectiveness in the performance of business functions. They are set up by the obligation to serve the public at a competitive price.

The general relations between business objectives may be summarized as follows: The primary objective of the business organization is an economic service. A profit is a personal objective of owners. Wages, salaries, bonuses, and related benefits are the personal objectives of executive and operative employees. Any personal objectives are necessarily collateral business objectives. There are many subclasses of these objectives. The accomplishment of any objectives must conform to accepted standards of business conduct.

Values must be created by work. Business objectives condition accordingly the work of the organization. They are the starting points of business thought and action. The determination and analysis of objectives involve forecasting. Many techniques for estimating and specifying the objective have been developed. Their importance suggests that further development of them may be expected.

An organization basically is any group of individuals who are cooperating to a common end under the guidance of leadership. A particular organization may be good, bad, or indifferent from the standpoint of objectives, policies, or any other criterion. A leader is anyone who accepts responsibility for the accomplishment of group objectives. He must usually discharge this responsibility to the satisfaction of the group. Otherwise, there may be a loss of morale and organizational effectiveness that may cost him his position. He is expected to motivate, coordinate, and direct the organization, or some element of it, in the achievement of its objectives.

Satisfactory accomplishment implies an effective, economical performance of both managerial and operative functions. The requirements and conditions of such accomplishment change as our society develops and our economy changes accordingly. There have been and are various kinds, grades, and conditions of executive leadership in business organizations. A great business leader who was successful in one era might not be successful in the next. The conditions of executive leadership under a war economy are different from those in peacetime. The founder of a business often lacks the executive ability to lead it successfully from its pioneer stage through the stage of exploitation to the stage of relative stabilization. Leadership that is successful during a period of inflation may be unable to lead the organization successfully through a period of depression. Positive leadership is usually more effective than negative leadership in the long run. There are times, however, when negative leadership is necessary for the successful handling of disciplinary cases or emergency situations. The leadership responsibilities of the administrative executive are related to but different from those of the operative executive. It is evident that any formula for continuing executive success must be open to question. There are principles of effective executive leadership. They are the principles of good management.

Administrative management is chiefly group management. Operative management is chiefly project management. The former is concerned largely with long-time projections of the activities of organizational groups. Operative management is concerned largely with short-time action in the execution of specific projects. Usually they must be accomplished with reference to time objectives in the immediate future. Other fundamental distinctions between administrative and operative management. . . account partly for the fact that many capable operative executives are unable to rise to top business leadership.

The big financial rewards are found in the echelon of top administrative management. They supply much of the incentives that induce bright, ambitious young men to strive for advancement in an organization. There is no easy road to success, however. These rewards are usually paid for inspiration rather than for perspiration. There is a high rate of obsolescence among executives who are too "practical" to keep abreast of the developing science of management.

Policy is a basic factor in business organization. A business policy is essentially a principle or group of related principles, and their consequent rules of action. They condition and govern the successful achievement of certain business objectives toward which they are directed. A principle is an expression of the relationships between cause and effect in a particular problem. It is a statement of these relationships that is accepted as a significant truth. A good statement of sound policy supplies, therefore, a cogent relationship between business objectives and ideals on the one hand, and organizational functions, physical factors, and personnel on the other. Sound policy is obviously a requisite for sound planning. A statement of policy, express or implied, is often found in the statement of a plan. Nevertheless, a policy is not a plan.

The policy-making function breaks down into certain definite phases. They are policy formulation, promulgation, education, acceptance, application, interpretation, and control. They are part of any executive job in some degree. Much of the top executive's time is spent on problems of general adminstrative policy. Such policies enter into long-range planning and the subsequent work of organizing. Rules, on the other hand, are restrictive. They enter into control. Even a minor operative executive occasionally makes rules for the guidance of operatives under his supervision. If not, he must interpret rules that have been made by his superior. These rules must be made within the framework of the broader policies that are originated on higher levels.

The intelligence with which policies are made and applied can stimulate or depress the morale of the organization. Unity of action depends on unity of thought. Effective accomplishment depends on unity of action. A common body of principle is an important factor in the development of unity of thought. There appears, in consequence, to be a growing tendency to commit important policies to writing in the form of policy manuals and rule books. There is also a tendency to link management's policy-making responsibilities more closely with the lower echelons of the business organization in which they are applied. Executives on operative levels are included in the work of policy formulation to a greater degree, through application of the Principle of Participation. Policy control in large organizations tends to be decentralized.

Business functions are the work of accomplishing the various objectives of the business organization. The nature and amount of this work depend on the characteristics and requirements of these objectives. Business is an economic institution. Its objectives are primarily economic. The mission of the business organization is to supply the portion of the public which it serves with certain goods and services. Structural and procedural planning for an organization rests necessarily on some theory of functionalization. Any such theory in business organization must rest on the concept of economic utility. Such utility may be defined as the ability of an economic good or service to supply the customer with the satisfactions of his needs or desires for which he spends his money. He may transfer his patronage to a competitor if he does not get these satisfactions in satisfactory amounts. The customer still has the right of freedom of choice in the market place. The attributes of the product or service that give it the required utilities are its quality attributes. They are so recognized in industry by marketing experts, engineering executives, and quality managers.

The organic functions of a business establishment are, therefore, the creation of economic utilities, the distribution of these utilities, and the provision of the capital that is necessary for the performance of the first two functions. They are the functions of production, distribution, and finance in a manufacturing establishment. They are different in other basic types of economic institutions, except for the common function of finance.

All chains of command within a business organization stem originally from one of its organic functions. They develop, by the processes of functional differentiation, with increasing business volume and consequent organizational growth. The devolution of a line organization leads directly downward to a division of operative work and specialization in the creation of primary service values. Finance is an exception to this statement. . . .A staff organization evolves from a line organization. It makes possible a division of managerial work and specialization in the creation of collateral or secondary service values. It may be appended to a line organization at any level where such managerial service is needed. It cannot be part of the line organization however. Both line and staff functions have their executive and operative phases. There are no distinctions between them in this respect. There are various distinguishing characteristics, of course. One simple test of a staff function is this: Does its devolution lead directly to specialization in the creation or distribution of salable values? If it does not, it is probably staff.

Functions must be grouped on a logical basis as they are differentiated from one another. This basis should permit the development of good cooperation, coordination, and leadership. There are various principles of functionalization that underlie structural and procedural planning. They have these objectives in view. Some functions are similar to one another. They have similar objectives, factors, and difficulties. They require for their performance personnel having similar background, training, experience, personality, and other attributes. We may group functions in accordance with these similarities. We may relate these groups by lines of responsibility and authority. The result is some form of organization structure. Some functions are complementary to one another. They produce values that are a prerequisite for other values that must be produced subsequently in accomplishing the mission. These functions may be grouped in steps in its accomplishment. They may be related to one another on the basis of their complementary nature, but with due regard for organizational lines. The result is some form of business procedure. All business functions have complementary and similar characteristics with respect to other related functions.

The complexity of functionalization necessarily increases as the volume of business grows. There is some evidence that this complexity tends to increase in geometric progression. Much of it is a result of staff organization growth. Staff contributes necessary collateral and secondary values. Otherwise the staff personnel would not be retained on the payroll. It is overhead expense, nevertheless. This suggests that there is an optimum size for a business establishment. Yet a rising standard of living requires increasing aggregations of capital and labor in some industries. "Bigness" in business organizations is not bad *per se*. If it were, the difficulty could not be cured by bigger state trusts that are run by governmental functionaries. The answer in business organization is usually some form and degree of economic integration and decentralization. It is not necessarily dissolution.

The problems of business functionalization are not simple. The design of organization structure and procedure has become, in consequence, an increasingly important part of the work of administrative planning in large organizations. Some good techniques for functional investigation and analysis have been developed. Some sound principles of functionalization have been established. Nevertheless, the subject can benefit from more research.

Effective performance, in any organized activity, requires a delegation of responsibility and authority. This is true for both executive and operative performance. Responsibility is an individual rather than a group phenomenon. It is the obligation that an individual acquires in any organization when he accepts an assignment of certain objectives, functions, and duties. An executive responsibility is an obligation to perform leadership functions under certain conditions. It necessarily involves the direction and supervision of others. An operative responsibility is an obligation to perform, to the best of one's ability, certain assigned duties, under executive direction, in the accomplishment of a particular project. An operative responsibility does not involve direction and supervision of the work of others. Authority is the term for the rights that are necessary for the satisfactory discharge of one's organizational obligations. Executive authority includes, therefore, the rights of decision and command with respect to the organizational activities of one's subordinates. Operative authority includes such rights of decision as are necessary for the proper performance of assigned operative duties.

Accountability is a condition of membership in an organization. It requires that each member must render a report of his discharge of responsibilities, and be judged fairly on the basis of his record of accomplishment. Such judgments rest on qualitative and quantitative evaluations of individual and group performance. These evaluations result chiefly from the performance of the control functions of supervision and comparison. They determine the extent to which the individual has accomplished the assigned objectives. The operative employee is accountable for the accomplishment of operative objectives that have been assigned to him. The executive employee is accountable for the results accomplished by the individuals and groups who are working under his direction. The principal phases of the problem are: (1) analysis of objectives, (2) functional analysis with respect to the requirements for the accomplishment of these objectives, (3) functional grouping and the division of responsibility as a basis for structural and procedural design, (4) determination of the authority required for each allocation of functions and responsibility, (5) the delegation of responsibility and authority, (6) the establishment of control, and (7) the development of accountability. Many problems are involved. The economy and effectiveness with which the organization accomplishes its mission depend on how well they are solved.

The division, allocation, and delegation of responsibility rest on whatever groupings of functions have been made. They may be line or staff. The ultimate unit function, in any case, is a single, simple act of operative performance, either mental or physical. It must have definite points of starting and stopping. This concept enters directly into the techniques of motion and time study. The motion principles associated with it enter directly into the design of organization structure, however. The ultimate unit of operative responsibility is the obligation of an operative employee to perform assigned duties within his job classification. It is based on the general work assignment that is set up in his job specification. The ultimate unit of executive responsibility is the unit of operative supervision. It is the number of units of operative responsibility that is suitable for direction and the exercise of face-to-face leadership by a first-level supervisory executive. Experience indicates that the size of this supervisory unit tends to range from ten to thirty operatives. The reasons have to do with the economy and effectiveness of supervisory leadership. There is also an effective, economical unit of executive supervision. Experience indicates that its size tends to range from three to eight or nine subordinate executives. The relations in organization structure between these units of operative and executive supervision have an important influence on the success of the organization.

The value of the contribution that an individual is required to make increases with the service level on which he works. There is some good evidence that it tends to increase in geometric progression. A given job is and should be worth more in a big concern than in a small one. The importance of the individual in organization success tends to vary inversely with organization size, nevertheless. The "indispensable men" are more likely to be found in small concerns than in large ones. The division and allocation of responsibility may be made in the former with respect to the individual ability and know-how of the present executive personnel. The supply of leadership material may be quite limited in the small organization. In the big concern, it may be made largely with respect to the requirements of functions for proper performance. Any modifications of sound organizational relationships to suit the inadequacies of present personnel are likely to be temporary. The large organization tends to have greater stability and permanence for these and other reasons.

A delegate is a person who is appointed to represent and act for another. Any subordinate, whether executive or operative, is in a sense a delegate of the superior executive to whom he reports directly. The process of delegation is one whereby certain of the executives functions, responsibilities, and authorities are released and committed to designated subordinate positions. Responsibility and authority are attributes of the job. Delegation enables an executive to extend his abilities beyond the limits of his personal powers. It makes possible a division of labor and the development of specialization, whether executive or operative. It may stimulate or depress organization morale, depending on how well it is done. It has other effects on the organization. It is, accordingly, an important managerial problem. There are various principles of delegation. An understanding of them is an important part of an executive's know-how.

Decentralization takes place when a higher central source of responsibility and authority assigns certain functions to subordinate individuals and groups. These functions may be managerial or operative, line or staff. Their decentralization is accomplished through delegation. Any assignment of functions to subordinates should be accompanied by adequate delegation of responsibility and authority. Otherwise the individual cannot justly be held accountable for results. There are various advantages and disadvantages of decentralization. There are various principles and conditions that govern the extent to which it is practicable. This extent tends to vary directly with the size of the organization. There are some obvious limitations, however. Delegation cannot result in the abdication of one's responsibilities and authorities. There is no direct relation between processes of delegation and the democratic process. The latter is a political concept. The business organization is an economic institution, under a condition of free enterprise and the right of private property.

Organization structure is the structure of relationships between groups of similar functions, physical factors, and personnel. These relationships have to do largely with responsibility, authority, and accountability. They affect organizational morale. It is possible, therefore, to have a good organization structure, a beautiful organization chart, and a poor organization. An effective, economical accomplishment of assigned objectives is not characteristic of poor organizations.

There are only two basic forms of organization structure: line and staff. All other forms are variants of them. The "line" is the primary form. It is the backbone of the organization. A primary hierarchy of functions leads directly from an organic business function to a division of primary operative labor. It is an effect of functional differentiation. It results directly in specialization in the creation and distribution of salable values. A primary chain of command is the hierarchy of responsibility, authority, and accountability that is related directly to the primary functional hierarchy. A primary line organization is the present hierarchy of individuals, both managerial and operative, who perform line functions. The necessary responsibility and authority for such performance should be delegated to their job assignments. All staff groups exist to serve the line organizations, or other staff groups, for this reason. The tendency in most business concerns has been to resist the transfer of line authority to staff groups. Such transfer tends to break down the line organization. It leads to the defeat of the enterprise in the battle of competition, as it approaches a condition of complete functionalization.

The growth and devolution of the line organization begins, theoretically, with the owner-manager. Some concerns have actually started from this point. It results increasingly in the grouping of primary operative functions on one or more of the following bases: (1) product, commodity, or service, (2) process or method, (3) equipment or other dominant physical factors, and (4) the physical dispersion of business activities on a geographical basis.

These functions must be grouped in units of operative and executive supervision. The relationships that should exist between these units are primary determinants of line organization form. The basic relationships between them can be expressed mathematically. Such relationships assist in the provisional determination of the number of major service levels or echelons that are needed by an organization. They help in determining general criteria of the number of line executives required by the organization at various levels. They underlie the solution of other organizational problems. An application of these relationships results in some interesting conclusions. Very few major echelons are required to command a very large organization. The percentage of line executives to primary operatives should increase very little with organization growth.

Top executive payroll is and should be insignificant, relative to the total payroll of the organization and the contributions of effective top leadership. Other significant conclusions may be drawn. It should of course be remembered that there is no mathematical substitute for executive judgment. A concern does not manage by formulas.

The structural form of the small organization is predominantly line. The characteristics of line organization make its use particularly advantageous in the small business. Its advantages may be lost with organizational growth. This will take place unless the line is supplemented increasingly with staff organization. Management must be decentralized increasingly without loss of control of the organization's activities. Lack of organizational know-how may limit the growth of the small business as much as the competition of big business, and possibly more.

Staff organization structure is an evolution from a primary functional hierarchy. It is made necessary chiefly by increases in the load of managerial work and increasing requirements for specialized background, training, experience, and ability. Hence it has to do with a division and specialization of managerial labor. It takes place necessarily above the level of operative performance. A staff organization, accordingly, assists the line and other staff organizations in the performance of some phase of an organic managerial function. It usually performs some facilitative services in addition. The nature, extent, and degree of staff performance are determined and limited by delegation.

The basic classification of staff functions must rest, therefore, on the classification of organic managerial functions. These functions are the creative planning, organizing, and controlling of the activities of organizational members in the accomplishment of a common objective. Technical staff functions assist the organization in planning. They may assist it by performing certain specialized functions that are purely facilitative. They may do both. They require a certain specialized background, training, and experience for their performance. They may or may not be professional, however. Coordinative staff functions assist the organization in control. They too may perform certain facilitative functions. Successful performance of staff control functions usually requires breadth of background, training, and experience, rather than intensity. There are no staff groups that specialize solely in organizing. It is unlikely that there will be. . . .

All managerial functions, whether line or staff, have their operative phases. This is evident, since all functional devolution leads to operative specialization, either primary or secondary. Staff objectives are principally secondary. Staff organizations supply values that the line organization must have for the accomplishment of primary objectives. The latter are certain utilities in goods or services. They enable the customer to enjoy the values for which he pays his money. It is evident that staff objectives and functions are necessarily secondary in incidence of service to the public. They are not necessarily secondary in the importance and value of their contributions, however.

Organizational growth, whether line or staff, tends to follow a typical structural pattern. It is helpful in analyzing structural problems, if it does not result in a formulistic approach to organizational planning. Any general pattern must be modified and adjusted to fit the realities of the particular situation. We saw, during the discussion of organization structure, that the assigned mission of a staff group, and the conditions under which it must be accomplished, govern the detailed form that this pattern tends to take. It is evident that the devolution of a technical staff function must lead to professional or other operative specialization in planning, when the principal objective of the staff group is certain types of plans. The engineering department is a classic example. The devolution of a technical staff function must lead to professional or other operative specialization in facilitation, when the principal objective of the staff group is facilitative assistance. The devolution of a coordinative staff function must lead to operative specialization in control. Such specialization must be based on the organic staff phases of control. Any supporting planning services or associated services of facilitation for any staff organization must be placed in a secondary technical staff function in business organization, regardless of how vitally important it may be and how great its development is in the particular concern. Any supporting control services also must be placed in a secondary coordinative staff position. Such a position means that the particular function is attached directly to a secondary chain of command in a staff relationship.

Any staff organization is overhead. There is nothing scientific about an elaborate, complicated, and expensive staff organization that is not needed. It is not good business on the other hand to refuse to spend money for staff organization that is needed.

The development and growth of staff organization results from the growth in the demand for the company's services. It is both a cause and an effect of business success. The development of staff services has to do largely with the development and expansion of the basic staff duties. These duties are (1) investigation, including research, (2) analysis of facts and information, (3) interpretation, including services of information, (4) recommendation, including the formulation of plans, (5) coordination, including assistance in control, and (6) facilitation, including assistance in organizing and executing plans. Such development often requires continuing staff evolution with business growth. The principal stages of staff evolution are (1) line integration, (2) distinct staff differentiation, (3) complete staff differentiation. (4) staff integration, (5) staff elevation, (6) staff decentralization, and (7) complete staff separation. It is not necessary that all staff development begin with the first stage. It is not necessary either that the development of all staff functions be carried through to the final stage. It is helpful in diagnosing present staff difficulties to be able to recognize the stage of development of the particular staff organization. One must of course know the basic requirements for staff economy and effectiveness that are associated with this stage. It is helpful in organizational planning for staff growth to know the subsequent stages and their requirements. Such knowledge should be part of the professional background of the modern executive. In too many cases, it is not.

There has been increasing interest, in recent years, in top administrative management. The importance of top leadership in rapidly changing situations is apparent. The desirability of relieving top executives of some of the burden of administrative management has been realized. Some interesting developments in the field of top administrative staff organization have taken place as a result.

A staff organization that assists the chief executive in administrative planning is concerned with interdivisional coordination of thought. It is concerned, therefore, with problems of top administrative organization structure, procedure, general policies and objectives, and the general condition of organizational morale. It has close relations necessarily with financial planning. It does not do the work of any major technical staff division. Such divisions are still responsible for the development of plans and policies for activities within their fields of specialization. A vice-president in charge of personnel and industrial relations, for example, is still responsible for developing and recommending personnel plans and policies. A staff executive for administrative planning merely achieves a meeting of minds between the immediate line and staff subordinates of the chief executive. Any resulting plans are subject to the latter's approval.

A staff organization that assists the chief executive in administrative control is concerned largely with interdivisional coordination. Much of the work at this level has to do with long-range planning. Accordingly, it is concerned with progress in the accomplishment of planning projects. It is concerned subsequently with the progress of the major divisions of the business in organizing for the execution of plans. It must evaluate divisional performance in the accomplishment of assigned objectives. Administrative control deals with the constraint and regulation of group action in the completion of administrative projects. These projects may extend over considerable time periods—a month, a quarter, a year, or longer. It is not concerned directly with the current execution of operative projects and their schedules. General administrative control performs its functions at the top administrative level of the organization.

There are a great many structural problems, such as the difficulties associated with functional emergence; the location of dissimilar staff functions; the duties, responsibilities, and authority of headquarters staff executives; the development of staff parallelism; the use and limitations of committees; and many others. They greatly affect the development of top administrative organization. Much more information concerning their characteristics and requirements would be helpful. The literature of business management deals largely with the discussion of technical and coordinative staff problems at the various levels of operative management. It is only in comparatively recent years that we have been getting some worth-while contributions from executives with practical experience in top administrative management. It is probable that the next great advance in managerial science will take place in this area.

The United States is committed to the policy that the standard of living of its people must increase continuously. An ultimate objective is the maximum average living standard that is practicable at any point in time. Progress has been uneven, with many temporary setbacks, for a number of reasons. They have to do with the errors of omission and commission of our economic and political leadership, the weaknesses of an industrial democracy that must be based on the right of private property, and many other factors that are well known. The result has been, nevertheless, a strong, upward growth trend in a dynamic, industrial economy. These objectives and policies place certain responsibilities on business for the maintenance of a corresponding growth in the number and size of the business establishments that serve our people. Such business growth inevitably creates many major organizational problems within the business establishment. These responsibilities require executives to understand the attributes of business organization that are required for growth. They are, in general, the attributes of good organization anywhere. The principal ones are (1) effective executive leadership, (2) sound business objectives and policies, (3) sound functional relationships as determined by objectives, (4) adequate physical implementation that will make possible an economical, effective accomplishment of objectives, (5) a complement of abilities, both executive and operative, to handle present business problems economically and effectively, (6) organizational stability, (7) organizational flexibility, (8) organizational capacity for growth, (9) organizational balance, and (10) good organizational morale.

The first five of these attributes were discussed earlier in this chapter. The remaining five require further comment. Organizational stability is the quality that enables an organization to adjust itself promptly to personnel losses without serious losses of economy or effectiveness. Organizational flexibility is the quality that enables it to adjust itself to temporary changes in business volume and conditions without serious losses of economy or effectiveness. Many concerns have done a good job of developing these organizational attributes. Most concerns appear to have done a poor job of developing capacity for growth. The exceptions are found usually among large, successful corporations. This attribute may be defined as the ability of an organization to adjust its personnel and structure to permanent changes in business volume, without serious losses of economy or effectiveness. It is concerned usually with the permanent expansion and development of the organization. This is likely to be a continuing problem, as long as our economy is expanding. Growth is a requirement, in some industries, for the maintenance of competitive effectiveness. Many concerns do not conform to the requirements of this definition, because they handle growth problems on the basis of short-range planning, trial and error, and expediency. Their weaknesses show up quickly when they are forced to expand to a large size quickly during a war emergency.

Some of the greatest failures of executive leadership have been in the field of morale. It has appeared, at times, as though anyone could take away from the executive the leadership of his employees by the simple expedient of offering something for nothing. It is possible that this has been another effect of too many business mechanics and too few professional executives who are capable of exercising economic statesmanship.

Morale is a mental condition of individuals and organizations. It determines their attitudes. As a result, it conditions the degree of acceptance of executive leadership by organization members. It governs the quality of their cooperation in the accomplishment of organizational objectives. Good organizational morale is a condition in which individuals and groups voluntarily make a reasonable subordination of their personal objectives to the service objectives of their organization. An industrial society can be overthrown by the destruction of the morale of its industrial organizations. There is an organizational Principle of the Primacy of the Service Objective. It says that an organization may fail when any important individuals or groups in it succeed in placing their personal interests ahead of its interests for any considerable period of time.

The morale-building process is, accordingly, a process of integrating interests. It is any process that develops and maintains identities and interdependencies between the organization's service objectives and the personal objectives of its members. The interests of individuals are most acute with respect to the values they desire for themselves and for those immediately dependent on them. The process has to do, therefore, with creating the conditions that will assure an adequate satisfaction of personal objectives. It must do this in a manner that is compatible with competitive effectiveness.

Confidence in the integrity and ability of executive leadership is an important condition for the successful operation of the morale-building process. There must exist some belief that the present subordination of personal interests to organizational interests will result in worth-while future benefits for the individual or group. The desired benefits may be tangible or intangible, or both. Surveys of employee interests have indicated, for example, that wages, hours and working conditions are not always the principal considerations of operatives. This may happen when employees in a particular organization generally regard the benefits associated with such considerations to be fair and adequate. Such surveys suggest that a feeling of worth-whileness, a feeling of belonging to an organization in which one can take pride, a feeling of security, or some other intangible value may be the thing that is desired.

The morale problem, like any other, must be broken down into its principal elements before a general method of approach to its solution can be devised. The following are the principal functions in the morale-building process: (1) analyses of individual and group interests and objectives and of their relation to organizational service objectives, (2) establishment of common concepts and yardsticks of value, (3) provision of values that are desired by individuals and groups in the organization in adequate and proper amounts, (4) prompt, equitable adjustments of conflicts between personal and organizational interests as they develop, (5) morale maintenance, including continuous identification of organizational and personal objectives.

No problems can be solved without adequate facts that are reasonably accurate. Various techniques for getting morale facts have been devised. They involve some form of intermittent or continuous morale surveys. The former are usually a statistical approach, based on the use of questionnaires. The latter are usually a qualitative approach, based on the use of trained observers. The most effective observers should be line supervisors, provided that they have been trained to do the job and have the ability. The most effective method for getting morale facts is likely to involve a combination of statistical and qualitative techniques.

A distinction between morale factors and morale effects should be made in applying any survey method. The attitudes of individuals and groups toward the organization and its leaders are obviously effects of their state of mind. They directly affect the economy and effectiveness with which the organization accomplishes its mission. Some of the more important effects of good morale are willing cooperation, loyalty to the organization and its leadership, good discipline, and organizational initiative. There are others. A morale index is a relative measure of the attitudes that indicate morale effects.

A morale factor is anything within or outside the organization that affects the personal interests of its members in relation to its own. We saw above that these interests include more than money. A morale stimulant is any factor that tends to produce favorable attitudes toward the organization and its leadership. A morale depressant is a factor that tends to produce unfavorable attitudes. It is possible for a particular morale factor to be a stimulant and a depressant at different times and under different circumstances. Some of the more common factors in good morale are worth-while organizational and personal objectives, good leadership based on a sound philosophy of management, homogeneity of group characteristics and interests, decentralization, indoctrination, satisfactory physical work environment, and many others. They should be determined and specified clearly, concisely, and in as much detail as is practicable.

The scale of values that individuals and groups in an organization apply to their interests is obviously an important factor in morale development and maintenance. It is an effect of their philosophy. It affects morale directly, insofar as it bears on the activities of the organization and its leadership. An outside agency has an opportunity to substitute a scale that suits its purposes when the organization's members have no philosophy of their own.

A philosophy is a body of doctrine. The latter term refers to any formal statement, either express or implied, of objectives, ideals, principles, points of view, and general modes of procedure. A doctrine is laid down for the guidance of others, either with or without the authority to compel its acceptance. It can relate to physical or psychical phenomena, or both. The purpose of a managerial philosophy is to make clear the significance of business concepts. It underlies the mission of rendering an economic service for producers and consumers. Proper indoctrination of its members is a leadership responsibility in any type of organization. Business organization is no exception. Complete indoctrination in a business organization is not proper, of course. It is practically impossible, so long as we retain the rights underlying freedom of press, freedom of speech, and freedom of assembly. It is not in the long-term interests of business executives in a competitive society. The process in the business organization is one of self-indoctrination. It is a process of education. . . .

Poor morale cannot be blamed successfully on professional labor leaders. Organizational morale is a responsibility of the organization's leadership. This is not an argument against collective bargaining. Free enterprise, collective bargaining, and individual liberty rest squarely on the right of private property. The destruction of any one of them tends to destroy the right of private property. The destruction of the right of private property tends to destroy them all.

Voluntary cooperation, an intelligent exercise of initiative, self-coordination, and similar values are effects of good morale. They reduce the degree and extent of control that is necessary. Good morale cannot be a substitute for good control, however, even in small organizations. Self-control breaks down quickly with increasing organization size. Increasing executive control must be developed with organizational growth. Otherwise, paradoxically, an organization may fail in accomplishing its mission as a result of its success.

It was noted earlier that the organic functions of management are the creative planning, organizing, and controlling of the activities of the organization's members in the execution of their assigned tasks. They are the functions of executive leadership. The function of control is the work of constraining and regulating such actions in accordance with plans for the accomplishment of specified objectives. The economy and effectiveness of execution and control depend directly on creative planning and organizing. The ultimate objectives of control are, of course, the ultimate service objectives of business. They are, therefore, better customer values. Control coordinates and correlates action in accordance with a plan for the accomplishment of such objectives. The immediate objectives of control are derived from the objectives of the particular plan. They are, in general, (1) assurance of correct performance as specified by the plan, (2) a well-coordinated condition of action, and (3) a minimum of losses due to interferences with the proper execution of the plan.

The two grand divisions of the work of executive leadership are administrative management and operative management. Each division has its line and staff phases. They may be completely differentiated and highly developed in large organizations. Staff functions may exist only potentially in the very small organization. A distinction must be made accordingly between operative control and administrative control. Operative control is chiefly project control. Administrative control is chiefly group control. It is the function of constraining and regulating group action in the completion of assigned programs. The latter summarize the results that are anticipated from the completion of assigned projects during a designated period of time. The cumulation of values resulting from the completion of these projects during this period provides a measure of the degree of accomplishment of organizational objectives. The latter were set up when the program was planned. The facts that are necessary for the operation of a system of administrative control come, then, from the reports originated by the system of operative control on the lower echelons.

Control on any echelon tends to break down into eight basic subfunctions. They are the organic phases of control. They are (1) routine planning, (2) scheduling, (3) preparation, (4) dispatching, (5) direction, (6) supervision, (7) comparison, and (8) corrective action. . . . [The] eight control functions tend to be performed in the order indicated. This temporal order is not mandatory, of course. However, it provides a useful basis for the analysis of control procedure. The line phases of control are direction, supervision, and corrective action.They cannot be differentiated from the line organization and assigned to staff groups, except to a very limited degree with respect to their most routine aspects. The reasons are found in their direct relations to line leadership responsibilities. The remaining five control functions may be assigned to staff control groups in a very high degree.

The extent to which control is exercised by subordinates is governed by the extent to which control responsibilities have been delegated and decentralized. Supervisory executives are responsible only for the line phases of control when the staff phases are highly centralized. They have certain responsibilities for morale maintenance that are inherent in the relation of face-to-face leadership. They have no control responsibilities if they have no obligations and rights with respect to direction, supervision, and corrective action. Their leadership position is undermined. They are not likely to discharge their morale responsibilities satisfactorily in such case. A centralized staff control sets up a completely functionalized relationship. It tends to concentrate responsibility and authority in the hands of higher line executives.

Differing degrees of centralized control may exist within one organization for the same function. The administrative control of production is highly decentralized down to the plant level in large concerns engaged in continuous manufacturing. It is highly centralized within the plant, down to and including plant stores and the production lines. The reasons are found in the principles of decentralization that have been discussed.

Just as morale conditions the quality of control, so control conditions the quality of morale. Disciplinary action, for example, is a phase of corrective action. Good discipline is an effect of good morale. It is a condition of voluntary conformity with policies, rules and regulations. The latter are necessary for coordinated and cooperative action in the accomplishment of group objectives. Good discipline is related to other morale effects such as willing acceptance of executive decisions, voluntary cooperation, and organizational pride. Disciplinary action is a managerial process for conditioning individual and group behavior. Its objectives are the inhibition of improper behavior, the integration of personal and organizational interests, and the assurance of correct action in the future. It accomplishes these objectives by means of penalties or rewards. Disciplinary action has to do, therefore, with the addition or substraction of certain values in the situation of an individual or a small group. It may be taken with respect to a person, but it should not be personal. The intent is usually to condition the quality of future action by the group of which the individual is a part.

Control may have other important effects. Their implications may go far beyond the limits of the particular undertaking that is being controlled. An understanding of the basic principles and significances of control is an important part of the background of the professional executive.

Business procedure is a basic factor in the performance of organizational functions. It is a relationship of complementary functions that is set up as a basis for the execution of a project. The latter may be managerial or operative. It may be line or staff. It must be planned, in any event, with regard for the requirements for the successful accomplishment of project objectives. It must consider the requirements for human and physical factors in performance, and the limitations of their use that must be observed. The specified procedure is an important part of a project plan, since it supplies a basis of action. The installation of standard procedures is often an important part of the work of organizing.

A procedure specifies, among other things, the order in which the various steps in the accomplishment of the project must be performed. It states the quantitative time requirements for the performance of each step, or indicates where such information may be obtained. A procedure necessarily cuts across organizational lines, because of the complementary nature of its functions. Coordination of action is a control responsibility. It has to do largely with the time and order in which the steps or phases of an undertaking are performed. Business procedure is therefore a basic factor in control.

The economy and effectiveness with which project and organizational objectives are accomplished depend greatly on the quality of procedural planning. The executive head of each group is responsible for developing and using the best methods for the accomplishment of his objectives. A mark of a good executive is ability to make effective use of staff, whether his own or others'. No one usually cares, within reason, how he develops the best methods, provided that he uses them. This concept brings up some interesting problems in line and staff relationships as the organization grows. They must be solved, if the organization is to enjoy continued success.

The objectives of procedural development are secondary values. The principal values are (1) orderliness in the execution of business undertakings, (2) consequent uniformity of results, (3) facilitation of specialization, (4) a more effective and economical utilization of personnel, (5) conservation of executive ability, time, and health, (6) facilitation of executive and self-coordination, and (7) economy and effectiveness in the performance of managerial and operative functions. Responsibility for developing a particular type of business procedure is often delegated to the staff group in whose special field the problem falls. It would be impractical for top line executives, for example, to concern themselves personally with the details of planning a top administrative procedure. This is too important, on the other hand, to be delegated to people with limited ability and then forgotten. The result of such action may be ineffectiveness, high cost, and red tape. A top staff executive for administrative planning can be given staff responsibility for coordinating thought concerning structural planning, procedural planning, and other problems of administrative planning. The scope of his responsibility must be limited to the top administrative echelons. He should be available for consultation when executives on lower echelons are unable to achieve a meeting of minds on their procedural problems. This may be an intelligent compromise. There is some evidence of a trend in this direction.

A profit is a legitimate reward of capital for the successful acceptance of business risk in rendering an economic service. It is necessary for the formation of private capital and the continuation of the free enterprise system. It is necessary for the maintenance of the right of private property, and in consequence the freedom of the individual. Ability to operate a business at a profit should not be the sole criterion of managerial excellence, however. A profit may be a legitimate objective of businessmen. It should not be the primary objective of a business organization. The objective of the latter is an economic service. There are collateral business objectives. Business operations vitally affect the public interest. The sum total of all goods and services produced and distributed by all business enterprises everywhere, great and small, approximates the total national income. It represents the material benefits that support a high standard of living in an industrial economy.

Management is a principal form of economic leadership. Accordingly, the executive in private business has a great public responsibility. This has been recognized increasingly by organized business. One effect has been the development of more professional executives. Their numbers are still too few, however. Their development has been limited by the evolution of a sound philosophy of management. This evolution has been taking place, of course. Such a philosophy will be needed badly if it becomes necessary to expand our industrial organizations quickly for war purposes. It will be needed for the preservation of our democratic institutions when the subsequent contraction of business activities takes place. It will be necessary for a further, sound development of our economy. . . .

4 Social Exchange Systems Theory

● The two theories in this chapter—those of Chester Barnard and of James March and Herbert Simon—are together because they are related. The work of March and Simon draws heavily from that of Barnard and there is a substantial degree of conceptual overlap.

There are, however, different points within each theory that have been the focus of those interested in organizational theory. For instance, Barnard's work is most often associated with the "acceptance theory" of authority, while March and Simon's work has often been referred to as a "decision approach" to organizations.

One of the primary thrusts in the attack on the classical theory is toward its treatment of authority, and many have used Barnard's treatment as the main weapon in their arsenal. Barnard has defined authority differently than the classical theorists. To Barnard, authority is not a right but rather the "character of a communication... by virtue of which it is accepted by a...member." The "acceptance approach" revolves around the necessity of assent of the individual, which will occur when

   1) the order is understood;
   2) it is in the individual's best interest to comply;
   3) the individual perceives it as consistent with the purpose of the organization; and
   4) he is mentally and physically able to comply.

These conditions will prevail if the order is within the individual's "zone of indifference." If all orders were ranked in their order of acceptability, some would be unacceptable, and would therefore not be obeyed. Other orders would be neutral. The remainder the individual would comply with. It is this last group of orders which fall in the zone of indifference. March and Simon have called this same concept the "acceptance zone."

There is no question about compliance, or the acceptability of an order, when it falls within this zone. The individual may act out of habit, or he may decide to comply because he fears the consequences of noncompliance or because he desires to satisfy a superior in order to obtain rewards of the system.

The width of the zone of indifference, according to Barnard, depends upon the subordinate's evaluation of the induce-ments/contribution balance. That is, the greater the individual perceives the surplus of inducements over contributions required, the wider the zone of indifference—and the boundaries of this zone may shift.

But Barnard is describing the "action" side of authority, or the case where one does, in fact, respond. Some have interpreted Barnard's position to mean that authority is "accepted." Actually, the lower participant is one link in an influence process that may be initiated at higher levels. Individuals acquiesce to these influence attempts because they fall within his zone. But what are the reasons for this, beyond the previously mentioned inducements/contributions assessments? Subordinates may respond when a superior acts in an official capacity. Officialness results from the position of the superior. Thus a position may impute a degree of legitimation to the communication. Barnard calls this the "authority of position," yet this is not a great deal different from the concept of authority described in the classical literature. Barnard's concept of authority is different, however, because he is defining it in terms of the response of the subordinate, not in terms of bases of power. Classical theory tends to emphasize primarily one basis, positional power.

March and Simon, in dealing with the "decision to produce," seem to follow closely Barnard's notion of acceptance theory. The individual's motivation to produce is a function of

1) the character and consequences of the evoked set of alternatives;

2) the values the individual compares these to;

3) group norms; and

4) formal policies and incentive practices.

March and Simon have refined, extended, and supported the hypothetical observations of Barnard by an examination of the empirical research evidence which supports the various propositions.

There are those who have argued that the acceptance theory of authority assumes free will on the part of the individual who is the object of the influence attempt. Krupp (14), for instance, argues that it implies "consent" and that the choice is "free." His use of "consent" and "free," we believe, sets an emotional tone to his argument which is unnecessary. Others, who have criticized the classical theory and subscribed to the acceptance approach, couch their arguments in terms of a democratic bias. Does the zone of indifference or acceptance mean that an individual responds because he wishes to? No, we may "accept," though grudgingly, directives that carry negative sanctions. One may not be happy, and may wish to leave the organization, but under these conditions acceptance must mean carrying out the request.

Let us turn briefly to the March and Simon formulation. This has been called a "decision approach" to organizations, but why is this so? March and Simon, and Barnard, devote a great deal of time to a discussion of the individual in an organization, as distinct from looking at the organization as the classicists did. They, and Barnard, posit that an individual in an organization is faced with two major decisions, the decision to participate and the decision to produce. These two decisions are affected by two different sets of factors. The decision to participate is based upon the concept of organizational equilibrium, or the inducements/contributions balance. The decision to produce is based on such factors as the individual's goals and values, his group affiliations, and the cues he receives from the internal and external environment.

The theories presented in this chapter are rich in hypotheses and ideas for those studying organizations. Many of Barnard's thoughts for instance, have found expression in other theories. Examine his discussion of the composition of formal organizations, for example. Organizations are made up of smaller organizations called "organization cells." The number of these cells increases because a leader is limited regarding the number of people with whom he can communicate. This notion is strangely reminiscent of "span of control." When an individual cannot communicate with a large number of people, organizational growth can occur only by grouping two or more of these unit organizations. This grouping needs a superior. Thus, as the number of unit organizations increase, there is a corresponding need for more superiors. Then groups of groups are combined, and so on. The leader of a group, or unit organization is a member of two groups; his own working unit in which he is a superior, and his own superior group in which he is a subordinate. This is not unlike the "linking-pin" concept generally attributed to Likert (16).

But these notions are expressed within the extracts and the summary/review that follow. In these an effort is made to link these concepts with other major elements of the theories—H.L.T.

The Functions of the Executive

CHESTER BARNARD

The individual possesses certain properties which are comprehended in the word "person." Usually it will be most convenient if we use the noun "individual" to mean "*one* person" and reserve the adjectival form "personal" to indicate the emphasis on the properties. These are (*a*) activities or behavior, arising from (*b*) psychological factors, to which are added (*c*) the limited power of choice, which results in (*d*) purpose.

The materials in this section generally are drawn from opening statements of passages which are carefully developed and explained in the original work. The purpose of the excerpt is to highlight main themes. The development of these themes can be found in the original work. Excerpted by permission of the publishers from Chester I. Barnard, *The Functions of the Executive*, Cambridge, Mass.: Harvard University Press, copyright 1938, 1968 by the President and Fellows of Havard College; 1966 by Grace F. Noera Barnard.

(*a*) An important characteristic of individuals is activity; and this in its gross and readily observed aspects is called behavior. Without it there is no individual person.

(*b*) The behavior of individuals we shall say are the result of psychological factors. The phrase "psychological factors" means the combination, resultants, or residues of the physical, biological, and social factors which have determined the history and the present state of the individual in relation to his present environment.

(*c*) Almost universally in practical affairs, and also for most scientific purposes, we grant to persons the power of choice, the capacity of determination, the possession of free will. By our ordinary behavior it is evident that nearly all of us believe in the power of choice as necessary to normal, sane conduct. Hence the idea of free will is inculcated in doctrines of personal responsibility, of moral responsibility, and of legal responsibility. This seems necessary to preserve a sense of personal integrity. It is an induction from experience that the destruction of the sense of personal integrity is the destruction of the power of adaptation, especially to the social aspects of living. We observe that persons who have no sense of ego, who are lacking in self-respect, who believe that what they do or think is unimportant, who have no initiative whatever, are problems, pathological cases, insane, not of this world, *unfitted for cooperation.*

This power of choice, however, is limited. This is necessarily true if what has already been stated is true, namely, that the individual is a region of activities which are the combined effect of physical, biological, and social factors. Free will is limited also, it appears, because the power of choice is paralyzed in human beings if the number of equal opportunities is large. This is an induction from experience. For example, a man set adrift while sleeping in a boat, awaking in a fog in the open sea, free to go in any direction, would be unable at once to choose a direction. Limitation of possibilities is necessary to choice. Finding a reason why something should *not* be done is a common method of deciding what should be done. The processes of decision as we shall see are largely techniques for narrowing choice.

(*d*) The attempt to limit the conditions of choice, so that it is practicable to exercise the capacity of will, is called making or arriving at a "purpose." It is implied usually in the verbs "to try," "to attempt." . . .We are greatly concerned with purposes in relation to organized activities.

It is necessary to impress upon the reader the importance of this statement of the properties of persons. . . . It will be evident as we proceed, I think, that no construction of the theory of cooperative systems or of organizations, nor any significant interpretation of the behavior of organizations, executives, or others whose efforts are organized, can be made that is not based on *some* position as to the psychological forces of human behavior. . . (pp. 13-14).

1) The individual human being possesses a limited power of choice. At the same time he is a resultant of, and is narrowly limited by, the factors of the total situation. He has motives, arrives at purposes, and wills to accomplish them. His method is to select a particular factor or set of factors

in the total situation and to change the situation by operations on these factors. These are, from the viewpoint of purpose, the limiting factors; and are the strategic points of attack.

2) Among the most important limiting factors in the situation of each individual are his own biological limitations. The most effective method of overcoming these limitations has been that of cooperation. This requires the adoption of a group, or non-personal, purpose. The situation with reference to such a purpose is composed of innumerable factors, which must be discriminated as limiting or non-limiting factors.

3) Cooperation is a social aspect of the total situation and social factors arise from it. These factors may be in turn the limiting factors of any situation. This arises from two considerations: (*a*) the processes of interaction must be discovered or invented, just as a physical operation must be discovered or invented; (*b*) the interaction changes the motives and interest of those participating in the cooperation.

4) The persistence of cooperation depends upon two conditions: (*a*) its effectiveness; and (*b*) its efficiency. Effectiveness relates to the accomplishment of the cooperative purpose, which is social and non-personal in character. Efficiency relates to the satisfaction of individual motives, and is personal in character. The test of effectiveness is the accomplishment of a common purpose or purposes; effectiveness can be measured. The test of efficiency is the eliciting of sufficient individual wills to cooperate.

5) The survival of cooperation, therefore, depends upon two interrelated and interdependent classes of processes: (*a*) those which relate to the system of cooperation as a whole in relation to the environment; and (*b*) those which relate to the creation or distribution of satisfactions among individuals.

6) The instability and failures of cooperation arise from defects in each of these classes of processes separately, and from defects in their combination. The functions of the executive are those of securing the effective adaptation of these processes (pp. 60-61).

It is [a] central hypothesis...that the most useful concept for the analysis of experience of cooperative systems is embodied in the definition of a formal organization as a *system of consciously coordinated activities or forces of two or more persons* (p. 73).

The system, then, to which we give the name "organization" is a system composed of the activities of human beings. What makes these activities a system is that the efforts of different persons are here coordinated (p. 77).

[a] If organizations are systems, it follows that the general characteristics of systems are also those of organizations. For our purposes we may say that a system is something which must be treated as a whole because each part is related to every other part included in it in a significant way. What is significant is determined by order as defined for a particular purpose, or from a particular point of view, such that if there is a change in the relationship of one part to any or all of the others, there is a change in

the system. It then either becomes a new system or a new state of the same system.

Usually, if the parts are numerous, they group themselves into subsidiary or partial systems. Where this is the case, each partial system consists of relationships between its own parts which can change, creating a new state of the partial system, without altering the system as a whole in significant degree. But this is true only when the system is viewed from a single or special point of view and the changes of the subsidiary system are within limits. When this is the case we may disregard the larger systems, treating them as constants or the subsidiary system as if it were isolated. Thus the whole physical universe is the single and fundamental system, consisting of parts—which, let us say, are electrons, neutrons, and protons—and relationships between them; but in practice, if our interest is narrow enough, we can deal with the solar system, or the sun, or the earth, or a piece of iron, or a molecule, or an atom, as if each were a complete and final system. This we can do if we do not exceed certain limits. These are determined by whether or not exceeding these limits involves important changes in, or important reactions from, the larger system.

This is similarly true of the systems called organizations. First of all each organization is a component of a larger system which we have called a "cooperative system," the other components of which are physical systems, social systems, biological systems, persons, etc. Moreover, most formal organizations are partial systems included within larger organization systems. The most comprehensive formal organizations are included in an informal, indefinite, nebulous, and undirected system usually named a "society." . . .

[b] But we must now refer to one question about systems in general, and about organization systems in particular, the answer to which is of fundamental importance. I refer to the question as to whether the whole is more than the sum of the parts; whether a system should be considered as merely an aggregate of its components; whether a system of cooperative efforts, that is, an organization, is something more or less than or different from its constituent efforts; whether there emerge from the system properties which are not inherent in the parts.

The opinion that governs [here] is that when, for example, the efforts of five men become coordinated in a system, that is, an organization, there is created something new in the world that is more or less than or different in quantity and quality from anything present in the sum of the efforts of the five men (pp. 77-79).

[c] It remains to present a few remarks on the dimensional characteristics of the system of cooperative interactions which we define as organizations. It perhaps has impressed many executives how indefinitely organizations are located in space. The sense of being "nowhere" is commonly felt. With the great extension of the means of electrical communication this vagueness has increased. To be sure, since the material of organizations is acts of persons, and since they relate in some degree to physical objects or are fixed in some physical environment, they have some degree of physical location. This is especially true of organizations in factories, or connected with railroad or communication systems. But even in

these cases location is indirect, by attachment to a system of physical things; and in the case of political and religious organizations even mere location is only feebly conceivable. The notion of spatial dimensions of these systems is hardly applicable.

On the other hand, the dimension of time is of prime importance. Temporal relationship and continuity are primary aspects of organizations. When and how long are the first items of description. . . . The persons whose acts are the components of these systems are continually changing, yet the organization persists (p. 80).

The theory of formal organization

An organization comes into being when (1) there are persons able to communicate with each other (2) who are willing to contribute action (3) to accomplish a common purpose. The elements of an organization are therefore (1) communication; (2) willingness to serve; and (3) common purpose. These elements are necessary and sufficient conditions initially, and they are found in all such organizations. The third element, purpose, is implicit in the definition. Willingness to serve, and communication, and the interdependence of the three elements in general, and their mutual dependence in specific cooperative systems, are matters of experience and observation.

For the continued existence of an organization either *effectiveness* or *efficiency* is necessary; and the longer the life, the more necessary both are. The vitality of organizations lies in the willingness of individuals to contribute forces to the cooperative system. This willingness requires the· belief that the purpose can be carried out, a faith that diminishes to the vanishing point as it appears that it is not in fact in process of being attained. Hence, when effectiveness ceases, willingness to contribute disappears. The continuance of willingness also depends upon the satisfactions that are secured by individual contributors in the process of carrying out the purpose. If the satisfactions do not exceed the sacrifices required, willingness disappears, and the condition is one of organization inefficiency. If the satisfactions exceed the sacrifices, willingness persists, and the condition is one of efficiency of organization.

In summary, then, the initial existence of an organization depends upon a combination of these elements appropriate to the external conditions at the moment. Its survival depends upon the maintenance of an equilibrium of the system. This equilibrium is primarily internal, a matter of proportions between the elements, but it is ultimately and basically an equilibrium between the system and the total situation external to it. This external equilibrium has two terms in it: first, the effectiveness of the organization, which comprises the relevance of its purpose to the environmental situation; and, second, its efficiency, which comprises the interchange between the organization and individuals. Thus the elements stated will each vary with external factors, and they are at the same time interdependent; when one is varied compensating variations must occur in the other if the system of which they are components is to remain in equilibrium, that is, is to persist or survive (p. 83).

Willingness to cooperate, positive or negative, is the expression of the net satisfactions or dissatisfactions experienced or anticipated by each individual in comparison with those experienced or anticipated through alternative opportunities. These alternative opportunities may be either persqnal and individualistic or those afforded by other organizations. That is, willingness to cooperate is the net effect, first, of the inducements to do so in conjunction with the sacrifices involved, and then in comparison with the practically available net satisfactions afforded by alternatives. The questions to be determined, if they were matters of logical reasoning, would be, first, whether the opportunity to cooperate grants any advantage to the individual as compared with independent action; and then, if so, whether that advantage is more or less than the advantage öbtainable from some other cooperative opportunity (p. 85).

Willingness to cooperate, except as a vague feeling or desire for association with others, cannot develop without an objective of cooperation. Unless there is such an objective it cannot be known or anticipated what specific efforts will be required of individuals, nor in many cases what satisfactions to them can be in prospect. Such an objective we denominate the "purpose" of an organization. The necessity of having a purpose is axiomatic, implicit in the words "system," "coordination," "cooperation." It is something that is clearly evident in many observed systems of cooperation, although it is often not formulated in words, and sometimes cannot be so formulated. In such cases what is observed is the direction or effect of the activities, from which purpose may be inferred.

A purpose does not incite cooperative activity unless it is accepted by those whose efforts will constitute the organization. Hence there is initially something like simultaneity in the acceptance of a purpose and willingness to cooperate (p. 86).

In other words we have clearly to distinguish between organization purpose and individual motive. It is frequently assumed in reasoning about organizations that common purpose and individual motive are or should be identical. With the exception noted below, this is never the case; and under modern conditions it rarely even appears to be the case. Individual motive is necessarily an internal, personal, subjective thing; common purpose is necessarily an external, impersonal, objective thing even though the individual interpretation of it is subjective. The one exception to this general rule, an important one, is that the accomplishment of an organization purpose becomes itself a source of personal satisfaction and a motive for many individuals in many organizations. It is rare, however, if ever, and then I think only in connection with family, patriotic, and religious organizations under special conditions, that organization purpose becomes or can become the *only* or even the major individual motive (pp. 88-89).

The possibility of accomplishing a common purpose and the existence of persons whose desires might constitute motives for contributing toward such a common purpose are the opposite poles of the system of cooperative effort. The process by which these potentialities become dynamic is that of communication. Obviously a common purpose must be commonly known, and to be known must be in some way communicated. With some exceptions, verbal communication between men is the method by which this is accomplished. Similarly, though under crude and obvious conditions not to the same extent, inducements to persons depend upon communication to them (p. 89).

The size of a unit organization being usually restricted very narrowly by the necessities of communication, it follows that growth of organization beyond the limits so imposed can only be accomplished by the creation of new unit organizations, or by grouping together two or more unit organizations already existing. When an organization grows by the addition of the services of more persons it is compelled, if it reaches the limit of size, to establish a second unit; and henceforward it is a complex of two unit organizations. All organizations except unit organizations are a group of two or more unit organizations. Hence, a large organization of complex character consists not of the services of individuals directly but of those of subsidiary unit organizations. Nowhere in the world, I think can there be found a large organization that is not composed of small units. We think of them as having descended from the mass, whereas the mass can only be created from the units.

Usually when two and always when several unit organizations are combined in one complex organization, the necessities of communication impose a super-leader, who becomes, usually with assistants, an "overhead" unit of organization. Similarly, groups of groups are combined into larger wholes. The most obvious case of complex structures of this type is an army. The fact that these large organizations are built up of small unit organizations is neglected in the spectacular size that ensues, and we often pass from the whole or major divisions to "men." The resulting dismissal from the mind of the inescapable practice of unit organization often leads to utterly unrealistic attitudes regarding organization problems (pp. 110-11).

In summary, we may say that historically and functionally all complex organizations are built up from units of organization, and consist of many units of "working" or "basic" organizations, overlaid with units of executive organizations; and that the essential structural characteristics of complex organizations are determined by the effect of the necessity for communication upon the size of a unit organization (p. 113).

Informal organizations and their relation to formal organizations

The purpose [here] has been to show (1) that those interactions between persons which are based on personal rather than on joint or common purposes, because of their repetitive character become systematic and organized through their effect upon habits of action and thought and through their promotion of uniform states of mind; (2) that although the number of persons with whom any individual may have interactive experience is limited, nevertheless the endless-chain relationship between persons in a society results in the development, in many respects, over wide areas and among many persons, of uniform states of mind which crystallize into what we call mores, customs, institutions; (3) that informal organization gives rise to formal organizations and that formal organizations are necessary to any large informal or societal organization; (4) that formal organizations also make explicit many of the attitudes, states of mind, and institutions which develop directly through informal organizations, with tendencies to divergence, resulting in interdependence and mutual correction of these results in a general and only approximate way; (5) that formal organizations, once established, in their turn also create informal organizations; and (6) that informal organizations are necessary to the operation of formal organizations as a means of communication, of cohesion, and of protecting the integrity of the individual (pp. 122-23).

[Earlier] it was shown that the primary aspect of cooperative systems was the effect of coordination of the activities of two or more persons on the overcoming of the limitations involved in the relations between the biological capacities of individuals and the natural environment. This coordination may proceed on one of two principles: on the principle of simultaneity of effort, or on that of efforts in series (p. 132).

Thus, in an important aspect, "organization" and "specialization" are synonyms. The ends of cooperation cannot be accomplished without specialization. The coordination implied is a functional aspect of organization. This function is to correlate the efforts of individuals in such a way with the conditions of the cooperative situation as a whole that purpose may be accomplished.

The way in which this correlation is accomplished is to analyze purpose into parts or detailed purposes or ends, the accomplishment of which in proper order will permit the attainment of the final objective; and to analyze the situation as a whole into parts which may be specifically coordinated by organization activity with detailed ends. These when accomplished become means toward the final attainment. The nature of this process and the function of specialization are of critical importance in the understanding of executive work.

A final observation may now be made. Since every unit organization in a complex organization is a specialization, the general purpose of the complex must be broken into specific purposes for each unit of organization. Since purpose is the unifying element of formal organization, it is this detailed purpose at the unit level that is effective in maintaining the unit. It is this purpose which must be accepted first of all in each unit in order that there may be units of which a complex may be composed. If this local or detailed purpose is not understood or accepted, disintegration of the unit organization follows. This is not more than an induction from my personal experience and observation, as is what now follows: and it is obvious in any event that much qualification for time elements and degrees of disintegration would be required for a complete statement.

Understanding or acceptance of the *general* purpose of the complex is not, however, essential. It may be, and usually but not always is, desirable as explaining or making acceptable a detailed purpose; and if this is possible it no doubt in most cases strengthens the unit organization. But in general complex organizations are characterized by obvious lack of complete understanding and acceptance of *general* purposes or aims. Thus it is not essential and usually impossible that the company should know the specific objectives of the army as a whole; but it is essential that it know and accept *an* objective of its own, or it cannot function. If it feels that the whole depends upon the achievement of this objective, which it is more likely to do if it understands what the whole objective is, the intensity of its action will ordinarily be increased. It is belief in the cause rather than intellectual understanding of the objective which is of chief importance. "Understanding" by itself is rather a paralyzing and divisive element (pp. 136-38).

...The individual is always the basic strategic factor in organization. Regardless of his history or his obligations he must be induced to cooperate, or there can be no cooperation (p. 139).

The net satisfactions which induce a man to contribute his efforts to an organization result from the positive advantages as against the disadvantages which are entailed. It follows that a net advantage may be increased or a negative advantage made positive either by increasing the number or the strength of the positive inducements or by reducing the number or the strength of the disadvantages (p. 140).

It will be evident, perhaps, without more elaborate illustration, that in every type of organization, for whatever purpose, several incentives are necessary, and some degree of persuasion likewise, in order to secure and maintain the contributions to organization that are required. It will also be clear that, excepting in rare instances, the difficulties of securing the means of offering incentives, of avoiding conflict of incentives, and of making effective persuasive efforts, are inherently great; and that the determination of the precise combination of incentives and of persuasion that will be both effective and feasible is a matter of great delicacy. Indeed, it is so delicate and complex that rarely, if ever, is the scheme of incentives determinable in advance of application. It can only evolve; and the questions relating to it become chiefly those of strategic factors from time to time in the course of the life of the organization. It is also true, of course, that the scheme of incentives is probably the most unstable of the elements of the cooperative system (p. 158).

...Authority is the character of a communication (order) in a formal organization by virtue of which it is accepted by a contributor to or "member" of the organization as governing the action he contributes; that is, as governing or determining what he does or is not to do so far as the organization is concerned. According to this definition, authority involves two aspects: first, the subjective, the personal, the *accepting* of a communication as authoritative..., and, second, the objective aspect—the character in the communication by virtue of which it is accepted (p. 163).

The necessity of the assent of the individual to establish authority *for him* is inescapable. A person can and will accept a communication as authoritative only when four conditions simultaneously obtain: (*a*) he can and does understand the communication; (*b*) *at the time of his decision* he believes that it is not inconsistent with the purpose of the organization; (*c*) *at the time of his decision*, he believes it to be compatible with his personal interest as a whole; and (*d*) he is able mentally and physically to comply with it (p. 165).

Naturally the reader will ask: How is it possible to secure such important and enduring cooperation as we observe if in principle and in fact the determination of authority lies with the subordinate individual? It is possible because the decisions of individuals occur under the following conditions (p. 167):

(*a*) There is no principle of executive conduct better established in good organizations than that orders will not be issued that cannot or will not be obeyed (p. 167).

(*b*) The phrase "zone of indifference" may be explained as follows: If all the orders for actions reasonably practicable be arranged in the order of their acceptability to the person affected, it may be conceived that there are a number which are clearly unacceptable, that is, which certainly will not be obeyed; there is another group somewhat more or less on the neutral line, that is, either barely acceptable or barely unacceptable; and a third group unquestionably acceptable. This last group lies within the "zone of indifference." The person affected will accept orders lying within this zone and is relatively indifferent as to what the order is so far as the question of authority is concerned. Such an order lies within the range that in a general way was anticipated at time of undertaking the connection with the organization (pp. 168-69).

The zone of indifference will be wider or narrower depending upon the degree to which the inducements exceed the burdens and sacrifices which determine the individual's adhesion to the organization. It follows that the range of orders that will be accepted will be very limited among those who are barely induced to contribute to the system (p. 169).

Authority has been defined in part as a "character of a communication in a formal organization." A "superior" is not in our view an authority nor does he have authority strictly speaking; nor is a communication authoritative except when it is an effort or action of organization. This is what we mean when we say that individuals are able to exercise authority only when they are acting "officially," a principle well established in law, and generally in secular and religious practice. Hence the importance ascribed to time, place, dress, ceremony, and authentication of a communication to establish its official character. These practices confirm the statement that authority relates to a communication "in a formal organization." There often occur occasions of compulsive power of individuals and of hostile groups; but authority is always concerned with something *within* a definitely organized system. Current usage conforms to the definition in this respect. The word "authority" is seldom employed except where formal organization connection is stated or implied (unless, of course, the reference is obviously figurative) (pp. 172-73).

Thus men impute authority to communications from superior positions, provided they are reasonably consistent with advantages of scope and perspective that are credited to those positions. This authority is to a considerable extent independent of the personal ability of the incumbent of the position. It is often recognized that though the incumbent may be of limited personal ability his advice may be superior solely by reason of the advantage of position. This is the *authority of position*.

But it is obvious that some men have superior ability. Their knowledge and understanding regardless of position command respect. Men impute authority to what they say in an organization for this reason only. This is the *authority of leadership* (p. 173).

The functions of the executive

. . . Functions of executives relate to all the work essential to the vitality and endurance of an organization, so far, at least, as it must be accomplished through formal coordination (p. 215).

Executive work is not that *of* the organization, but the specialized work of *maintaining* the organization in operation (p. 215).

. . . The problem of the establishment and maintenance of the system of communication, that is, the primary task of the executive organization, is perpetually that of obtaining the coalescence of the two phases, executive personnel and executive positions (p. 218).

The second function of the executive organization is to promote the securing of the personal services that constitute the material of organizations.

The work divides into two main divisions: (1) the bringing of persons into cooperative relationship with the organization; (2) the eliciting of the services after such persons have been brought into that relationship (p. 227).

The third executive function is to formulate and define the purposes, objectives, ends, of the organization. It has already been made clear that, strictly speaking, purpose is defined more nearly by the aggregate of action taken than by any formulation in words; but that that aggregate of action is a residuum of the decisions relative to purpose and the environment, resulting in closer and closer approximations to the concrete acts. It has also been emphasized that purpose is something that must be accepted by all the contributors to the system of efforts. Again, it has been stated that purpose must be broken into fragments, specific objectives, not only ordered in time so that detailed purpose and detailed action follow in the series of progressive cooperation, but also ordered contemporaneously into the specializations—geographical, social, and functional—that each unit organization implies. It is more apparent here than with other executive functions that it is an entire executive organization that formulates, redefines, breaks into details, and decides on the innumerable simultaneous and progressive actions that are the stream of syntheses constituting purpose or action. No single executive can under any conditions accomplish this function alone, but only that part of it which relates to his position in the executive organization.

Hence the critical aspect of this function is the assignment of responsibility—the delegation of objective authority (p. 231).

Organizations as Viewed by James March and Herbert Simon

HENRY L. TOSI

The literature about organizations is basically the result of the experience of executives, the scientific management movement, sociologists, social psychologists, political scientists, and economists, little of which has been well substantiated empirically. Until recently, much organization theory was developed by the "classical" school, and this has been directed largely into two areas. The first is "scientific management." Theorists such as Taylor and Gilbreth brought a great deal of precision into the analysis, management, and reorganization of routine tasks. They attempted to develop a prescribed set of operating procedures to be used in analyzing and setting forth guide lines for effectiveness in organization.

The second category might be termed the "administrative management school." These writers were generally concerned with the most effective way to group tasks in order to achieve organizational purpose, dealing with problems such as how to group tasks into jobs, jobs into larger administrative units, these administrative units into larger units, and so on so as to minimize the cost of performing these activities. In general, these theorists attempt to develop principles of organization to be applied across organization types.

These theories were untested. The motivational assumptions they make about men and work tend to be inaccurate. There is little appreciation of intraorganizational conflict. By and large they may be criticized for their

The material analyzed here is drawn from James G. March and Herbert Simon, *Organizations,* New York: John Wiley, 1958. I am indebted to the publisher and the authors for permission to use it and I assume full responsibility for the interpretation herein.

lack of consideration of the human factor. They give little attention to the role of cognition in task identification, nor does the concept of program elaboration receive much attention. It is with these limitations regarding classical organization theory that March and Simon begin their work.

Some assumptions

An organization is a system of interrelated social behaviors of a number of participants. While the definitions generally used by the classical school fall within this construct, March and Simon derive their conclusions from the model of influence processes in organizations.

Behavior results from a stimulus. Stimuli are perceived by the individual. They act upon memory. Memory is composed of values, perceptions, beliefs, experiences, programs, alternatives, and other knowledge stored in the psychological bank of the individual. As a result of perceiving an external change in the environment, or stimuli, the individual evokes, or calls, for certain of these stored values or perceptions which he believes particularly pertinent to the situation. This "evoked set" contains some behavior program which the individual will enact. The "evoked set" is that part of the memory which influences the behavior of the individual. Memory content may move from an unevoked state, and so on.

Behavior can be changed, or influenced, in at least two ways. First, behavior may be changed by learning or changing the memory set of the individual. Then, in reacting to stimuli, the individual may evoke part of the new memory content. This, then should impact his behavior. Second, changing the stimuli may change behavior. Different stimuli may evoke different sets, which include different behavior programs, resulting in different behaviors.

There are several alternative outcomes that may occur using this influence model. First, the stimuli may act upon the memory and may obtain the desired behavior. Another possibility is that the stimuli is misunderstood by the individual and may evoke a different set than originally intended. The resulting behavior may be undesired. For example, a person may perceive an unintended stimulus; that is, changes in the environment whch were not planned by one who might have some control over it. This perceived stimuli may then evoke a certain set and perhaps trigger responses other than those intended.

In classical theory, most of these possibilities were overlooked, or not dealt with. The classical theorists did not consider in detail the fact that stimuli may generate unanticipated consequences because they may evoke a larger, or a different, memory set than expected. They believed that the environment contained well-defined stimuli which evoked a predictable memory set. This included a program for generating the appropriate, or desirable, response. For instance, use of the concept of economic man may result in offering increases in economic well-being to the employee, or organization member, as a stimulus. This presumably would evoke a set which contained values oriented toward improving one's economic status, a belief that such improvement is desirable, and a behavior program which includes the "appropriate" response of engaging in the activity desired by the management.

Organization equilibrium: The decision to participate

The individual in an organization is essentially faced with two different decisions. The first is the decision to participate, and the second is the decision to produce. These reflect different considerations by the individual. The *decision to participate* is based on the concept of organization equilibrium which refers to the balance of payments to members for their continued participation and contribution to the organization. The underlying concepts of organization equilibrium state that:

1) The organization is a system of interrelated social behavior of participants.

2) Each participant and group receives inducements from the organization for their contribution.

3) The individual continues to participate so long as the inducements he receives are greater than his contribution. This evaluation, incidentally, may be measured by the individual in terms of his own values, which may reflect or include those other than economic.

4) The contributions of various groups are sources from which the organization manufactures inducements to pay the others.

5) Equilibrium (or solvency) occurs when the organization can continue to provide inducement to members to obtain their contributions.

The individual and subgroups may be any groups or individuals which make some sort of contribution to the existence of the organization. In short, anyone providing input needed by the organization for its continued existence and survival must be viewed as an integral part of the system. Should one group leave, or change basically in nature, then the organization's equilibrium is disturbed, and a new level must be sought and achieved. This may require a redistribution of inducements to others in order to obtain their participation. The general scope of the concept of organization equilibrium considers managers, employees, customers, suppliers, investors, the communities, and lenders. The March-Simon structure could be slightly modified to apply to each of them. It has been common practice, however, to deal with the questions of membership in terms of employees and managers of organizations. March and Simon stay within this tradition.

The basic notion of organization equilibrium may be stated as follows: Increases in the balance of inducement utilities over contribution utilities decrease the propensity of the individual to move; decreases in the balance of inducement utilities over contribution utilities conversely increase the propensity to move. Inducement utilities received by an individual or group represent more than economic consideration such as wages. Satisfaction with the organization, identification with group members, and other noneconomic values all contribute to the inducement-contribution balance.

This balance is affected by two major considerations. These are (1) the perceived desirability of leaving the job, and (2) the perceived ease of movement from the organization. The perceived desirability of leaving is a function of the individual's satisfaction with his job and the possibility of intraorganizational transfer. When individual job satisfaction is high, it may be less desirable for one to move. There are a host of factors which affect job satisfaction (such as compatibility of work requirements with other roles, conformity of the work roles with the individual's self-characterization, and the predictability of instrumental relationships on the job), and when the individual is not satisfied with his job, he may consider the possibility of an intraorganizational transfer. If this possibility is high, then there is less likelihood of leaving the organization. Intraorganizational transfer possibilities may be related to the organizational size; that is, in large organizations there is a greater possibility of internal transfer than in small.

The second factor involved in the inducement-contribution balance is the individual's perceived ease of movement, or the number of alternatives he feels to be available to him. The more job offers he believes he has, the greater he perceives his ease of movement to be. Personal characteristics, such as sex, age, and social status may affect the degree to which he perceives external alternatives to be available. His skill and his increased length of service in an organization reduce, perhaps, the external alternatives he perceives available.

Thus, the likelihood of the individual leaving must be regarded as a function of his desire to leave and his perceived ease of movement. If he has no desire to leave, then perceived ease of movement is not important. If he is highly dissatisfied with the organization and does wish to leave, but he has few perceived external alternatives available, then it is highly likely that he will decide to remain in the organization—or participate.

The decision to produce

The decision to participate is based upon a set of different factors than those for the *decision to produce*. The motivation to produce is a function of the character of, and the perceived consequences of, the evoked set of alternatives. These are weighed against the individual's goals and values. The evoked set of alternatives evolves from the cues the individual perceives within the environment, both internal and external to the organization.

One factor which affects the decision of an individual regarding his organizational activities may be the perceived external alternatives. It may be more desirable to leave the organization than to comply with the production requirements or group norms. The factors involved in the individual's evaluation of these external alternatives have been discussed earlier. A second factor, the work group and its norms, also affect the individual's evaluation of alternatives. One evaluates alternatives in terms of group norms, or those behaviors which the group may define, acceptable. Thus, behavior of those in close social and physical proximity affect alternatives one may consider.

Formal organization practices, appraisal systems, compensation systems and management policies may elicit types of behavior which may, in fact, be considered organizationally undesirable. For instance, some managers may forego required short-run maintenance expenditures in a department in order to produce short-run results. The behavior elicited, and the evoked set of which it is a part, represent organizational problems that must be solved.

By and large, these alternatives represent action that an individual considers to be possible behavior. They do not emerge in a vacuum. We simultaneously consider behavior possibilities and evaluate, or assess, the perceived consequences of the evoked set. Conformity to organizational requirements will be less important when the individual perceives that he has other alternatives to participation in the organization, which may be largely determined by his perception of the job market or general labor market conditions. It is also a function of his perceived ease of movement to other organizations. When the individual feels that it would be difficult for him to move, that few jobs are available, he may view organizational conformity as important. He may also perceive only limited alternatives to participation and thus conform.

The degree to which the desired alternatives violate organizational requirements is another important individual consideration in the evaluation of alternatives. Effective compliance with organizational requirements is intended to result in the attainment and acquisition of organizational rewards. The reward-sanction system in an organization will have an effect on activity of members. Obtaining organizationally-based values is largely a function of an individual's ability to meet the performance requirements of the organization.

It is difficult to determine organizational performance criteria. These criteria may be a function of work group size; that is, the larger the work group, the more difficult it is to develop performance criteria and apply incentive systems. Second, the degree to which activities have been routinized and measured are an important dimension in criteria development. Organizational level is relevant here. Activities at the lowest level of the organization are more routine and programmed than higher-level activities. Operational criteria are generally more difficult to determine for higher-level officials. It may be extremely difficult to tie organizational rewards to current performance at high levels. For example, the success of an organization today may be a result of decisions made three, five, or ten years ago by some other chief executive, yet it is the incumbent chief executive who receives praise.

Identification with internal or external groups affects one's evaluations of the consequences. Group pressures will largely be a function of the degree to which the individual identifies with the group. The stronger the group identification, the greater the potential group pressures.

Group pressures are significant for other reasons, also. Group consensus or opinion uniformity, and the extent to which the group controls the environment, represent pressures that may have an impact on the individual even though he may not identify with the group. If the group is able to influence organizational activity, or control the reward-sanction system, the individual may be forced to respond to group pressures even though he does not identify with the group.

When an individual perceives a stimulus to engage in behavior, a set is evoked which includes alternative actions. Each of these alternatives is evaluated in terms of its perceived consequences. They are compared to some values, or standards, which are a function of the individual's goals. These do not develop in a sterile environment. Humans, in general, evaluate their own positions in relation to the values of others and may accept other's goals as their own. Individual goals emerge from the process of identification with others. Here the concern is with the degree to which groups of one sort or the other affect and condition the goals of the individual.

An individual may identify with any or all, at different points in time, of the following types of groups. First he may identify with professional associations, family, or other types of extraorganizational groups. Second, he may identify with friendship groups and other social-emotional subgroups within the organization environment. Third, he may identify with the organization itself. Finally, task groups in the organization involved in the performance of specific organizational assignments, similar perhaps to departments, may be the identification focus. Obviously, the stronger the group identification, the more likely it is that individual's goals will conform to those prescribed by group norms. These, then, are the factors related to group identification:

1) The greater the perceived prestige of the group, the stronger the propensity of the individual to identify with it. Prestige may be a function of success, status, or the individual's perception.

2) The greater the extent to which perceived goals are shared by members, the greater the identification with the group.

3) The more the perceived goals are shared by group members, the greater interaction of members.

4) The more frequent the interaction among members, the greater the propensity to identify with the group.

5) The greater the number of needs satisfied in the group, the greater the propensity of any individual to identify with the group.

6) The amount of competition between the individual and the group is negatively related to the degree of individual identification with the group.

Group conflict

March and Simon separate the decision to produce from the decision to participate. Simply because one elects to remain in an organization and operate at a given activity level, internal conflict and bargaining among members and member units are not precluded. The inducements/ contributions balance is flexible and the level of productive activity is elastic. This permits the degree of latitude within which organization conflict and bargaining can occur. The decision to produce and to participate may be within the range of "semi-conscious" motivational factors but conflict is more a "conscious and deliberate power phenomenon."

Conflict among organizational units arises from the following factors: the existence of a "felt need for joint decision-making," differences in goals, and differences in perceptions of reality. Individuals may feel that certain decision-making situations call for representatives from several units. There may be a high degree of instrumental interdependence among units.

Unit A may perform an operation on a product which may limit or condition the degree of success of Unit B. For instance, if Unit A is a metal-finishing department and Unit B is a paint shop, then the metal finish may significantly affect the quality of the paint job. Mutual dependence upon limited resources may increase the need for joint decision-making. Where several units rely on a limited budget for support, it is likely that members desire to jointly determine budget allocations.

Differences in perceived goals may be a condition that precedes conflict. Different organizational units may perceive different ends as justified. Organizational units may view their function as being more significant than other units, justifiably believing they should have a larger share of resources. Differences in goals may be a function of the size of the unit, particularly when it is reflected in the existence of a greater number of departments, which results in a larger number of differentiated goals.

Individual perceptions of reality may foster intergroup conflict. There may be great variance among the goals of individual members. The departmental affiliation of a member may alter his perception of problems. The kind of information and the communication channels through which it flows affects the perceptions of the reality of the problem. As the number of communications channels increases, the possibility for increased differentiation of perception within the organization occurs. When the same information passes through many different channels, each may distort, filter, and edit it to suit its own needs.

These factors lead to intergroup conflict. When conflict exists, it must be resolved to obtain equilibrium. Organization conflict may be resolved by analytic or bargaining processes. Analytic processes are those methods where public and private agreement among the conflicting groups is sought. Problem-solving and resolution of conflict by higher level officials are *analytic* processes. These tend to be used when the conflict situation is more a function of individuals than intergroup differences. The general characteristic of these processes is increased information of alternatives and evaluation of the consequences of them.

Bargaining processes are attempts to resolve conflicts through the use of "politics" or "gamesmanship." These techniques are predominant when the nature of the differences is between groups rather than individuals. Bargaining processes, however, require the use of power and status. This may have a negative impact on members. Power and status differences may be strengthened or weakened in the process. In either event, one group may suffer. Hence, there will be a tendency to treat conflict as "individual" and resolve it using an analytical method.

The cognitive limits of rationality

The classical concept of the "rational" decision-making situation is somewhat limited in practice. Rational, or optimum, decisions require that all alternatives to a problem are perceived by the problem-solver. Criteria must be available which permit these to be evaluated and compared. The alternative finally selected should be that preferred above all others.

This is hardly the case in organizational life, where it is unlikely that all alternatives are known. It is even less likely that criteria exist for adequate comparison of all alternatives. Thus, decision-making can only be rational within certain limits. The known alternatives, then, represent the boundaries, or parameters, of decision rationality.

Rather than "optimizing" as an organizational decision-making methodology, decision makers "satisfice." An alternative is considered satisfactory if (1) a set of criteria exists that describe minimally satisfactory alternatives, and (2) the alternative in question meets or exceeds all these criteria. Most human decision making, whether individual or organizational, is concerned with the discovery and selection of satisfactory alternatives. Only in exceptional cases is it concerned with the discovery and selection of optimal alternatives.

Decision making may be of many types, ranging from a case in which an individual searches for various alternative behaviors to one where an environmental stimuli invokes a highly complex and organized set of responses. These highly complex sets of responses are called "programs." The existence of programs accounts, in large part, for the predictability of individual performance and behavior. Programs may be viewed as a part of the organizational control system. Individuals in the organization accept programs based on the factors discussed previously under the "decision to produce."

Programs exist as a function of the ability to group activities and a need for coordination. When it is relatively easy to observe and relate job output and activities, then it is possible to develop programs. As the difficulty of observing this relationship increases, the difficulty of devising organizational programs increases. Programs may also exist, or be developed, when there is a need for coordination of either activity or output. Where there is a need for a great deal of coordination, then some method will be developed to insure that it occurs.

Programs are not meant to be extremely rigid behavioral specifications in all cases, but they may be. For instance, a program which prescribes behavior for an emergency breakdown of a production line may be highly specific. On the other hand, a program dealing with price determination of special job-lot produced equipment may be relatively flexible. Individual discretion in the use of programs is determined by whether it specifies outcome, or ends, to a greater degree than it specifies the means of achieving these ends. Programs which describe how to do something allow less discretion than programs which simply state the results desired. The hierarchical structure of programs within the organization is related to the concept of organizational levels. Higher-level officials in an organization modify programs implemented by lower-level personnel.

The organization's structure may be viewed as a function of the problem-solving process. The existence of structure, or programs, provides boundaries or parameters of rationalities for the decision-making process. Its existence provides some degree of stability and permanency to behavior within an organization, and this is a necessary characteristic of an organization behavior.

Rational behavior rests upon the concept of "goal." The individual defines his behavior in terms of goal attainment. Selection of alternatives which enhance the probability of obtaining goals may be viewed as rational behavior. Thus, the goals of the individual condition whether his behavior is "rational" or "irrational." The behavior of one unit may be viewed by another as being nonrational behavior because of discrepant goal perception. This may be due to factoring organizational views into subgoals for lower-level units.

Goal factoring may be viewed as a type of means-end analysis. If the overall organizational goal is viewed as the end, then those units at the highest level engage in the means of achieving that end. When one of these units is subdivided into small organization components, the means of the larger unit become the objective (or the end) of the smaller unit. This continues until such a condition exists that the overall organizational goal has been factored into small behavioral components. The factoring of overall organizational goals may result in units directing attention to its own goals. The degree of goal differentiation is important, since members of units often see goals in some particular frame of reference. Thus the number of departmental units, and the one with which an individual is affiliated, affects his goal perception.

As the goal becomes factored at lower and lower organizational levels, specialization of function and labor occur. Specialization of labor allows the organization to take advantage of repetitive programs. The type of specialization of labor, or the manner in which the goals have been factored, will affect the interdependence relationships among various departments. For instance, the greater the process specialization, the greater the interdependencies among departments.

The interdependency and complexities that can occur within an organization are limited by the effectiveness of the communication processes and channels. The communication channels, or systems, in an organization are both planned and spontaneous. Certain methods for transmission of specific types of information must be provided to satisfy formal organization requirements. Additionally, there may be a need for information that is not specifically sanctioned formally. Where this information gap exists, a channel will develop to provide it. The greater the efficiency in communications, the greater the tolerance among members for departmental interdependence.

The innovation and elaboration of programs

When the structure of active programs does not contain any which are adequate to meet organizational criteria, then they will be initiated to solve the problem. Programmed activity involves routine problem-solving. The details of behavior are relatively well-defined. Changing old programs, or devising new ones, requires a process of innovation and initiation. New program possibilities must be generated and their consequences examined. This innovative process is closely related to "problem-solving processes." In searching for programs, variables within the control of the individual, or the organization, will be first considered. If a satisfactory program is not developed, then an attempt will be made to change variables not within the discretion of the problem-solvers. If this fails, then the criteria may be relaxed.

The criteria for satisfactory performance are closely related to the pyschological concept of "level of aspiration." Aspiration levels change, but in general the adjustment process is a relatively slow, though constant one pressing upward. The aspiration level may be based on past organizational performance, but other bases of comparision also exert pressures. Firms compare themselves to other firms. When there is an awareness that better results can be obtained with other programs, there will be a revision in the standards of satisfaction.

The rate of innovation is likely to increase when changes in the internal or external environment make existing programs unsatisfactory. These environmental changes may result from design, or by accident. A "natural" process of innovation, that is, a response to environmental stimuli, may be supplemented by organizational mechanisms to facilitate innovation. Whether or not members engage in research for new programs is a function of time pressures or deadlines attached to activities, and the degree to which clear goals can be associated with the activities.

The discovery, development, and implementation of a new program in the organization may result in the creation of a new unit to develop, elaborate, and implement it. The development phase of new programs may be a period of high activity and excitement, while the implementation phase tends to spur less interest since the program is becoming more routine. New programs may be invented, or borrowed. If a program exists outside the boundaries of the innovating organization, then it is likely that the organization will "borrow." When such is not the case, organization members will first call on their "stored" program solutions. As more people in the organization become aware of the problem, the number of available solutions will increase. The development and elaboration of these new programs is through the process of means-end analysis. The solution to the general problem is by a set of generally specified means. Each of these means becomes a subgoal, and a set of means must be discovered for achieving it. This process continues until the level of detail is such that programs exist to achieve the subgoal, for which criteria must be developed. Sensitivity to innovations is a function of the relevance of the innovation to needs of the specific unit involved. When the goal of the innovation does not "fit" with that of the reviewing organization level, it is less apt to receive high priority, or it may be referred to the appropriate level. The location of innovation is important to the power and influence structure of an organization. Organizational activity is affected by the processes that originate and evaluate proposals. The right to initiate is a source of power. It is one control over organizational activities.

March and Simon's work—*Organizations*—is described by the authors as one in which they "surveyed the literature on organization theory, starting with those theories that viewed the employee as an instrument and physiological automaton, proceeding through theories that were centrally concerned with the motivational and affective aspects of human behavior, and concluding with theories that placed particular emphasis on cognitive processes."

5   Structural Systems Theory

● Amitai Etzioni develops a typology of organization and examines how individual involvement with an organization and the type of power predominant in the various forms interact to explain compliance. He is concerned with why people respond in organizations and, rather than relying on concepts of "acceptance" or property rights, he describes several different bases for compliance. Essentially, he argues that the type of power that will result in compliance is contingent on the nature of the organization and why people are there.

He does not focus on authority in the traditional sense but rather develops it more fully as part of the notion of compliance structure. Compliance is related to power means and the orientation of the individual. It is the behavior of the individuals responding to power, and power may take many forms, for example, material, deprivation, and so on. Etzioni argues that it is too narrow to view legitimated authority as the reason why people comply—that nonlegitimate authority affects behavior.

Power may be grouped into three types: (1) coercive—based on physical sanctions; (2) remunerative—based on control of economic resources; and (3) normative— based on manipulation of symbolic rewards. When the individual views organization efforts to obtain compliance as legitimate and/or congruent with his expectations, he will comply.

But individuals may be involved in organizations in different ways. Etzioni suggests these may be characterized as (1) alienative, (2) calculative, and (3) moral. He says that "There are nine possible types of compliance. Three of these types (congruent types) are more effective than the other six. . . . Organizations are under pressure to be effective. Hence to the degree that the environment allows, *organizations tend to shift their compliance structures from incongruent to congruent types and organizations which have congruent compliance of structures tend to resist factors pushing them toward incongruent structures* (9)."

Etzioni, then, as others whose work is included in this book, finds the concept of authority as a right inadequate to explain compliance behavior. More important, however, is the manner in which Etzioni attempts to relate the notions of authority, or compliance, and different types of organizations—H.L.T.

Etzioni's Theory of Organizational Compliance

R. J. HOUSE

Following is a summary/review of a theory of complex organization which has been developed by Amitai Etzioni.[1] The term "organization" as used here refers to a social unit devoted primarily to the attainment of specific goals.[2] Organizations as discussed here are complex in that they involve many levels, specialization of efforts, departmentation of groups within the organization, the need for both formal and informal communication and coordination and intricate relationships of authority and responsibility. This is a study of the systematic differences among various social units classed as organizations. The theory is diagrammed in Figure 1

Compliance as a base for comparison

In this theory, organizations are classified on the basis of their "compliance structure." Compliance is defined as a relationship consisting of the power employed by superiors to control subordinates and the orientation of the subordinates to this power. Thus, this theory combines a structural and a motivational aspect: structural, since it concerns the kind and distribution of power in organizations; motivational, since it concerns the different commitments of the members to the organization. In this theory, Etzioni seeks to analyze organizations in terms of both social systems and personality systems.

The basic assumption underlying the theory is that there are three major sources of control, whose allocation and manipulation account to a great extent for the foundation of social order within organizations. These control sources are: (1) coercion (threat and punishment), (2) economic assets (remuneration), and (3) social and moral values (recognition, acceptance and moral involvement). Accordingly, three types of compliance serve as the basis for comparison between organizations. Compliance—the organizational equivalent of social order—is the core variable, or hub, of this theory.

Power and involvement: The comparative dimensions

Using compliance as a comparative basis of analysis, organizations are analyzed in terms of two basic dimensions: *power*, which is applied by the organization *to* its members; and *involvement* in the organization developed *by* its members.

Involvement   **Type of Organization**

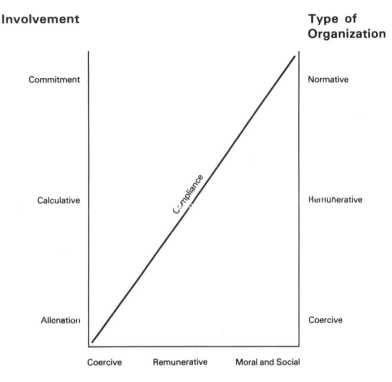

Figure 1. Power

Power. Power is referred to as a member's ability to induce or influence another member to carry out his directives by any other values which he supports. Power differs according to the means employed to make the subjects comply.

Thus, remunerative power is based on control over material resources and rewards through allocation of salaries and wages, commissions and contributions, "fringe benefits," services and commodities.

Moral and social power[3] rest on the allocation and manipulation of symbolic rewards and deprivations through employment of leaders, manipulation of mass media, allocation of esteem and prestige symbols, administration of ritual, and influence over the distribution of social acceptance and positive responses by others (e.g., recognition or approval). Thus, moral or social power rests upon the manipulation of those rewards which carry high symbolic value to the respondent.

Coercive power rests on the application, or threat, of physical sanctions such as infliction of pain, deformity, or death; generation of frustration through restriction of movements; or controlling the satisfaction of needs such as those of food, sex, comfort and the like through force.

Etzioni marshals evidence which strongly supports the proposition that most organizations tend to emphasize only one means of power, relying less on, but not completely avoiding, the other two. Most organizations, then, have both a primary and a secondary compliance structure.

Involvement. The second dimension of the theory is that of involvement. Involvement is characterized in terms of intensity and direction. The intensity of involvement ranges from high to low. The direction is either positive or negative. When involvement is high, it is called commitment; when it is low, alienation. Involvement thus is a term which applies to a continuum of personal and voluntary orientation toward an organization.

Classification of organizations

Etzioni classified organizations according to their compliance structure as coercive, remunerative, or normative.[4]

Coercive organizations. Coercive organizations are organizations in which coercion is the major means of control over the members, and high alienation characterizes the orientation of the members to the organization. Examples of coercive organizations would be prisoner-of-war camps, concentration camps, the large majority of prisons, traditional "correctional institutions," custodial mental hospitals, forced labor camps, and relocation camps.

Remunerative organizations. Remunerative organizations are those in which material remuneration is a major means of control over the members. This involves a determination by the member of the amount of involvement he feels will profit him most. Thus, "calculative involvement" characterizes the orientation of the members to the remunerative organization. Those divisions of industrial organizations employing predominantly blue-collar workers or white-collar, nonprofessional workers (clerks and stenographic workers) and semiprofessional workers such as laboratory technicians and most college graduates would be placed in this category. This is true because wages, salaries, commissions, fringe benefits, working conditions, and similar rewards constitute the predominant source of control for such employees. This placement of most industrial workers into the remunerative category of organizations is in agreement with the conclusions of Stogdill[5] and Brayfield and Crockett[6] that attempts to increase performance by changing the style of supervision to a more human-relations-oriented style are in some cases reported to lead only to small increases in productivity, whereas in other cases they cause an increase in employee satisfaction but none in productivity. On the other hand, reports from industry and surveys by government bureaus generally attest to the effectiveness of wage-incentive plans in increasing productivity and achieving other objectives, assuming that such plans are not in conflict with the moral values of the employees.

White-collar employees are predominantly controlled by remunerative means, but less so than blue-collar employees. Secondary, normative control, such as the manipulation of status symbols and social recognition seems to play a more important role among white-collar employees than among blue-collar employees.

Since white-collar employees have a greater tendency toward identification with the organizational objectives, and since management usually finds it difficult to manipulate esteem and prestige symbols of blue-collar workers, the use of social and moral values for purposes of influencing most industrial employees is limited.

A study of salesgirls by Lombard[7] points out behavior usually considered typical of lower-level workers. He reports, for instance, that the work groups restricts "output," limits competition among the girls, and enforces other norms which are in direct contrast to those supported by management.

At the same time, the manipulation of esteem and prestige symbols, which as a rule has a limited effect on blue-collar workers, seems to be more effective among white-collar employees. This point is illustrated in a study of salesgirls which emphasized the role of nonremunerative "symbolic" controls. Salesgirls who made mistakes writing out sales slips had the slips returned to them, bound with a large red rubber band, to be opened and corrected in the presence of the section manager and other salesgirls. These red bands "do not result in fines or punishments of any sort, and yet the clerks feel that to get one is a disgrace."[8] Similarly, there were "all sorts of honors bestowed upon the capable and efficient. These have small monetary value, but money is secondary to honor. To be ace—the best saleswoman in your department—is compensation enough in itself." [9]

One can imagine what the effects of similar manipulation would be if attempted with the blue-collar nonskilled worker. It is not unlikely that the person who gets the most red rubber bands would be the "ace of the day."

Normative organizations. Normative organizations are those in which moral involvement and social acceptance is the major source of control. The orientation of members of these is characterized by high commitment to the organization. There are several frequently found types of normative organization. These are religious organizations, employing primarily professional employees such as research laboratories, law firms and medical associations. In these kinds of organizations, social power is exercised mainly through informal sanctions (e.g., social isolation or approval), through the manipulation of prestige symbols (titles, status trappings), through the personal influence of the leader or influential members of the organization, or through the manipulation of peer groups' climate of opinion.

An organization made up of professional employees utilizes mainly moral and social controls, though calculative involvement occurs here to a greater extent than in any other kind of normative organization. In this sense, professional organizations resemble white-collar industries as borderline cases, though it seems they fall on the other side of the border, whereas in professional organizations moral and social power predominates, with remunerative compliance a close second. In white-collar industries the reverse seems to be true.

Today, with increased stress placed on creative scientific work, industries find normative, or moral social control affecting larger segments of their member population. Typically, industrial firms consist of a large portion of production people who are motivated primarily by remunerative means and a small but critical, and probably growing, portion of employees who are contributing toward the creative development of the product. The same is true of newspapers which have a highly remunerative section in which the newspaper is actually produced, and a highly committed, editorial wing in which it is written and edited. The editoral group may be more affected by normative power than the other sectors. Other communications industries, such as radio and television networks and advertising agencies, also have these characteristics.

The major means of control in professional organizations are based on prolonged and careful selection, education in professional value systems at universities and professional schools, or education on the job which the professional holds in the early part of his career. Examples of such jobs are the cub reporter, the law student, the intern, the novice, and the seminarian. Frequently, incumbents of these positions continue their professional education as part of the job, or on a part-time basis. Social powers, formalized in the professional code of ethics and the professional association and supported by the social bonds of the professional community and professional elites, carry great weight.

High intrinsic satisfaction from work, positively associated with voluntary involvement, characterizes the work of professionals. This commitment is sometimes disassociated from the organization and vested in the work itself, for which the profession—not the organization—serves as the reference group and the object of involvement. Thus, research scientists may be more easily persuaded by senior members of their discipline than by the managers of the firm. As one would expect from the comparatively extensive use of remunerative rewards, despite the importance of intrinsic satisfaction and other symbolic gratifications, commitment to professional organizations is not as high as it is in other normative organizations with strongly ideological overtones, such as some political parties or church organizations.

Leadership, compliance, and organizational specialization

Etzioni's theory has significant implications for management selection, the study of leadership, and organization. Organizations are often compared to task-performing, goal-oriented instruments. However, organizations which are seemingly committed to one set of goals must often pursue quite different subgoals or tasks in order to achieve those goals. These different goals and tasks frequently differ in their compliance requirements. Rarely are there two goals which can be served with optimal effectiveness by compliance structures which are precisely the same in both the predominant element and the weight given it.

It is because of the relationship between goals and compliance that multigoal or multitask "organizations" face a dilemma. Consistent emphasis on one pattern of compliance perhaps appropriate for one sector of the organization will cause a loss of effectiveness in the other because the pattern is congruent with only one task. If equal stress is given to two patterns or more, effectiveness may be reduced through neutralization.

However, segregation of tasks and/or personnel allows organizations to combine various compliance structures without losing effectiveness. Segregation may take the form of departmentation, thereby allowing different subunits of the organization to operate at the same time with relatively independent compliance structures. Or segregation may take place on the basis of time requirements. At any given point in time, the unit is employing only one compliance structure, but at later points in time it may switch to another. An example of this form of compliance is found in the military. During combat more reliance is placed upon moral-social pressures than during peacetime activities.

Etzioni argues that successful leadership within an organization depends upon the leader's ability to gain compliance. Ability to gain compliance depends upon the control relationship between two levels; that is, the power applied and the kinds of involvement of the members, rather than on the substance of the work carried out. Therefore it is possible that the compliance requirements of a situation may be more important than the technological considerations of the task. This suggests that the character of compliance should be considered, as well as, or even prior to, the division of labor on the basis of task specialization. Etzioni does not deny the advantage of independent task specialization—he feels that such specialization is important, but that it should take place within major constraints imposed by the demands of the compliance structure.

There have been two opposing viewpoints concerning effective control of organizational performance. One point of view holds that each control relationship is a distinctive specialty to be defined in terms of performances which are controlled. The nature of the control relationship is dictated by the executive's intimate knowledge of the tasks and performances he supervises. A different position is taken by those who suggest that the control function is universal and abstract. From this point of view, control always means the ability to obtain performances through other people. The main skill required is the ability to direct the work of others and get work done by getting other people to do it. Specialized knowledge comes from experts or staff positions, not from the executive. Thus, one position maintains that control is a highly specialized function, the other that it is highly general.

Etzioni postulates that "the control function is less specialized than the performance function, it is not universal in the sense that a person who is an effective control agent in one structure will be equally effective in others. . . ." "Control differentiation is *not* based directly on the kind of performances which are supervised, but on the kind of compliance effective performance requires." Styles of leadership (here, Etzioni refers to modes of control) should be differentiated according to the kind of discipline the leader must attain, and not according to the nature of work supervised, though the two are, of course, related to some degree. Stated another way, Etzioni suggests that "the effectiveness of the mobile executive is limited to compliance areas rather than administrative or technological boundaries."

Each type of compliance requires a distinctive set of personality characteristics, aptitudes, and inclinations. An individual may not have the characteristics required for more than one type of compliance. Thus, one would not expect effective combat leaders also to be effective "desk executives." Similarly, one would not expect a shop steward to be equally effective during periods of industrial harmony and in periods of labor-management conflict.

Footnotes

[1] For a more thorough discussion of this theory, see Etzioni, Amitai, *A Comparative Analysis of Complex Organization* (New York: Glencoe Free Press, 1961).

[2] The writer has taken the liberty of describing this theory in terms other than those used by Etzioni.

[3] In the original work, Etzioni refers to this kind of power as "normative power."

[4] In the original work, organizations are classified as "coercive," "utilitarian," and "normative." Utilitarian organizations are called "remunerative" organizations here.

[5] See Stogdill, R.M., *Individual Behavior and Group Achievement,* (New York: Oxford Press, 1959).

[6] Brayfield, A. H. and Crockett, W. H., "Employee Attitudes and Employee Performance" *The Psychological Bulletin,* September 1951, pp. 396-424.

[7] Lombard, G. F. F., *Behavior in a Selling Group* (Boston: Graduate School of Business Administration, Harvard University, 1955), pp. 124-30.

[8] Donovan, Frances R., *The Saleslady* (Chicago: University of Chicago Press, 1929), p. 64.

[9] *Ibid.,* p. 192.

6 Technological Systems Theory

● Much of the criticism of classical theory has been directed at its apparent insistence on the "one best way" of organizing and managing. The principles of management and the subsequent interpretation of such notions as span of control and authority and responsibility relationships were so often violated in the everyday practice of management that they could not be called "principles." Organizations simply do not operate the way that classical theory says they should. Thus, partly due to the inadequacy of classical theory, but also because of more intensive analysis, an obsession developed in some quarters about the limitations, and the eventual demise, of organizations which approximated bureaucracy.

To Victor Thompson, the bureaucratic model is inadequate; his focus is on the problem of conflict in organizations. To him, the traditional bureaucratic structure is not compatible with rapidly developing technology, hence conflict emerges between those with the responsibility for performance and those with the capacity to make decisions.

Thompson describes outcomes of a condition in which the authority of superiors is decreasing in legitimacy, while that of the specialist is increasing. For Thompson, authority in the hierarchy revolves around the question or the questions of rights and prerogatives of office. It is basic to his approach that bureaucratic authority be considered as a right of office, and similar to that presented in classical theory.

His argument is that the basis on which this right has been allocated—that is, presumed technical competence—is not appropriate. Decisions are shifting from the administrator to the specialist, yet the administrator is still held responsible. He posits a rigidity in organization structure which precludes adapting to that change, and since the structure is unlikely to be altered, and given the ever-growing gap between the right to decide and the ability to decide, the rigid structure results in a situation in which conflict is inevitable. Yet in order to maintain appearances of legitimate authority, defense mechanisms, Thompson argues, are used by both subordinates and superiors. These defense mechanisms resort to ideology, dramaturgy, and bureaupathology.

What Thompson presents is a dialectic dealing with power equalization in organizations that occurs when organization members are unwilling to accept the idea of legitimation and/or when the members operate in a rigid bureaucratic structure that will not change.

Sensitivity to changing technology and structural flexibility are organization conditions mandatory for effective integration of the authority and influence system in the official structure of an organization. Technology, with its concomitant increase in the number and type of specialists, generally is absorbed into the organization from external sources. This suggests that in industries or organizational groupings in which there are rapid developments and obsolence of technology, intraorganizational conflict and structural adjustment will be more critical to effectiveness than in cases where technology develops more slowly and predictably. Rapid technological change, of course, reduces the ability to predict future needs. This condition, in and of itself, implies a need for readiness for adaptation and change both in the technical and social system within the organization, but Thompson does not describe in detail alternative forms of organizations. This is done by the contingency theorists in chapter 7. Nor does Thompson describe mechanisms by which this adaptation occurs. This also will be done by the theorists in the next chapter.—H.L.T.

Victor Thompson's "Modern Organizations"

HENRY L. TOSI

Victor Thompson defines bureaucracy as a highly rationalized, impersonal integration of a large number of specialists operating to achieve some objective, upon which is superimposed a highly elaborate hierarhy of authority. The problem with which the organization must cope is securing the cooperation of specialists, and fitting specialization into a hierarchal framework. The individual is a cog in a large machine and loses some control over his destiny. He must respond to the organization. In many cases, the desired organizational response and that of the individual are opposite and problems arise.

In organizations there is a growing gap between the right to decide and the ability to decide. The right to decide is usually vested in a person performing a hierarchical role. On the other hand, the person with the greatest ability in the decision area may be performing a specialist's role. As specialization increases, this gap between the specialist and the administrator also increases. This theory is basically an analysis and an examination of the conflict between the hierarchical role and the technical role in organization and the consequences of this conflict.

The general characteristics of a bureaucracy

Modern organizations have emerged from earlier forms in which specialization was based on technical concepts. In early organizations, the superior usually had the ability, skill, and knowledge to make decisions. Today, by and large, the superior has *lost the ability to command, but not the right to command.* As the skills required to make decisions increase, the superior is unable to maintain a high skill level, since he must concern himself with other problems.

It is specialization which results in many characteristics which we commonly associate with bureaucracy, or formal organization. As organizations grow in size, the members of the organization must be grouped into units. These units are then grouped into larger units in order to accommodate specialization and coordination. According to Thompson, the characteristics of a bureaucracy are:

1) *Rationalism.* Organizations usually seek to solve problems in the most rational manner. They are concerned with decisions which will help them achieve the organizational goal. This emphasis on rationalism in organization is largely a reflection of the increasing influence of the specialist.

2) *Appointment by merit.* In large organizations, it is necessary to promote and appoint on the basis of merit if one is to rely on highly trained specialists. To insure that the individual will stay with the organization, he must be promoted on the basis of how well he performs within his specific set of work activities.

3) *Routinization of activities.* Within organizations, activities are broken down into groups of related routines which allow the specialist to engage in the performance of his specialty.

4) *Factoring of goals.* The organizational goal is viewed in a general sense. It is broken down and factored. These, then, become the objectives, or goals, for smaller administrative or departmental units. These goals in turn are broken down and factored until concrete routines are reached. These subgoals are assigned to the lower level and become their goals. This allows lower-level units to evaluate their activity in terms of more specific criterion, rather than in terms of the general goal of the organization.

5) *Apparent inversion of ends and means.* Usually, specific activities are assigned to units. Department, or unit, members must be concerned with the performance of these activities. When other organization members view these activities, it appears that the department members are overly concerned with the performance of those activities and the means for performing them, rather than the ends, or the objectives, which the activities are designed to achieve. For example, those who observe a budget office frequently accuse budget officers of believing the organization exists for the purpose of operating budget procedures.

6) *Formalistic personality.* Within large organizations there are few

close personal relationships among members. It is most likely that total involvement rarely occurs in interpersonal relationships.

7) *Categorization of data.* In order for the specialist to perform his activities and carry out his routines, it is necessary that he have data, and this data must be grouped into categories because of its quantity.

8) *Classification of people.* By and large, people in organizations are classified into subgroups. These subgroups, or classes of individuals, permit equal justice in policy application. Classification limits discrimination.

9) *Seeming slowness to change.* One of the major characteristics generally associated with bureaucratic organization is a tendency to react slowly, or to change slowly. This is partially due to the existence of specialists within the organization. It took time for them to acquire their skills and knowledge, therefore they may resist change which threatens them. This resistance is a kind of "cultural lag." People resist change because it upsets formal relationships and threatens the specialist with obsolescence.

10) *Concern with the monistic ideal.* In large organizations, there is a tendency to be concerned with the legitimation of the superior-subordinate relationship. Authority-responsibility relationships are stressed. The monistic emphasis is an emphasis on hierarchy. The pyramid is the resulting structure of organization that is described by the monocratic theory. The ideal application of the monistic model precludes the legitimacy of organizational conflict, divergent goals, and divergent interests of members. Since these conflicts are not legitimate, it is essential that administrators and managers spend time attempting to secure a "smooth-running organization."

As stated earlier, Thompson's analysis revolves around a study of the specialist role and the hierarchical role. The basic incongruities between these two roles and the resulting organizational consequences require discussion.

The specialist role

A bureaucracy is composed of specialized tasks developed from social processes. There are two types of specialization. The first is task specialization, a process of making activities more specific. It has to do with the division of labor. Task specialization is responsible for the repetitiveness of jobs. It occurs when an activity is subdivided into various component activities. These component activities then are grouped in some manner and assigned to an individual. Task specialization is an organizational process. It is somewhat less than completely desirable, however, since it results in limited meaning in the work to an individual.

A second type of specialization is personal specialization. It is a social process by which an individual adapts to his environment. Personal specialization makes the individual more powerful. The specific tasks he performs may be less specialized. When performance of less specialized tasks is required—that is, when the work to be done is less than routine—the result may be the specialization of the person who performs the task. Thus, the person will become a specialist. The specialization of people is a social process, prompted by the individual's welfare.

Personal specialization meets individual needs and contributes to social cohesion. Jobs which do not meet individual needs are not likely to contribute to social cohesion. Thus, highly specialized tasks, or repetitive work, may not result in great degrees of cohesion. Where there is a high degree of personal specialization in an organization, the members are forced to recognize the interdependence of one member upon others.

As suggested earlier, one of the problems in organization is to secure the cooperation of specialists. Where personal specialization has occurred within an organization, the members are required to recognize the necessary interdependence. Where interdependence is not viewed as being necessary by members, then it must be maintained by organization power. Thus, interunit relationships may be maintained by the recognized need of members, or the exercise of organization power.

Individual activities in organization are called "programs." These are organized sets of activities that are goal-directed. The individual can only learn limited numbers of them. Therefore, when new programs or activities become necessary for survival of the organization, new specialist positions within the organization must be developed.

Certain programs are combined into "instrumental relationships" to achieve externalized goals. Problems of the organization are reduced to a means-end map for solution. These problems are factored until they are reduced to a set of concrete programs. Programs are then grouped into jobs. These jobs must contain enough activity to keep their performers busy, but not so many different activities as to confuse them. The combination of programs into jobs must take into consideration the goals of the organization, the number of programs, and the extent to which the jobs fit into a supervisory unit. The number of ways that programs can be combined into jobs is limited only by the ability to perceive the possible relationships involved.

These same considerations apply to departmentalization, that is, grouping jobs into units, a unit into larger units, and so on. The kinds of departments in the organization are a function of the processes of specialization; they are the "instrumental relationships," or the exercise of hierarchical power to establish and maintain interdependencies. As tasks become more and more specialized, there is increased need for coordination. Because there is a tendency to emphasize the monistic concept of organization, relationships between specialist departments may be specified which are not in fact required. These relationships must then be supported by the use of authority.

The specialist may take many years to develop his skill. The fact that he possesses skill suggests that he may be most competent in making decisions in his skill area. Some decision-making may be passed from managers to specialists, however, and as this occurs and increases, the manager's job becomes more and more an exercise of authority without the skills necessary to make the decisions.

The hierarchical role

The hierarchy is a system of superior-subordinate roles and positions in the organization. In society, roles generally change in harmony with cultural changes. In organizations, particularly large complex bureaucracies, the advancement in specialization has brought pressure for hierarchical change. This pressure for change has been resisted, however, and, according to Thompson, the present emphasis in organization is still on the monistic concept.

In the hierarchy, the superior has certain rights. These are cultural role definitions. He may veto suggestions or proposals of subordinates. He may determine whether or not a proposal set forth by a subordinate should be implemented or forwarded to higher organizational levels. The subordinate generally has only limited rights of appeal. Obedience and loyalty of subordinates are also culturally defined rights that superiors may expect. The superior in a hierarchy generally expects his subordinates to comply with his directives. He has the right to monopolize communication between his unit and other organizational units, as well as the outside world. In general, he is responsible for communicating with higher-level officials regarding activity in his unit as well as transmitting directives from higher levels to his own unit. He has, as a result of his position in the hierarchy, a certain degree of status. He is also entitled to deference from his subordinates.

The essential nature of the rights of the superior is autocratic. He usually has the prerogative of selecting personnel within the unit, settling conflicts, determining goals of the unit (within parameters set by higher-level units) and may create nonhierarchical authority. This type of authority is a condition in which a superior may order a subordinate to comply with the influence attempts or the directives of other persons than himself.

The subordinate's role, on the other hand, is chiefly characterized by a set of duties. These duties are the correlatives of superior's rights. The subordinate's role generally requires recognition of the rights of the superior. It should be noted, however, that in most hierarchical roles, the subordinate is a superior of others. Thus, the subordinate in one relationship may be the superior in another. He therefore must concern himself with both the rights of a superior and the duties of a subordinate.

A great deal of hierarchical role behavior is concerned with deference and prestige. The hierarchy of deference in an organization is the status system. Status in an organization is important and signficant when considered in conjunction with the organizational distributive system. Satisfactions, beyond market minimums, are distributed to members according to the status system. The entrance to high-status position is controlled by the hierarchy. Thus the hierarchy controls positional assignments, as well as the satisfaction and rewards that members receive. These satisfactions and rewards are distributed in a skewed fashion. Those in top positions receive a great deal more than those in bottom positions.

The amount of prestige attached to a position increases at a rapid rate as one proceeds up the organizational echelons. Prestige associated with a position is disproportionate to its absolute level. Subordinates may accord increased prestige to higher-level positions for many reasons. A subordinate may admire the boss in order to protect his own self-image. Because of the lack of hard criteria to apply to superior's role performance, the evaluation is difficult. The ambiguity attached to higher-level roles increases their prestige, suggesting that in some cases the status and prestige accorded to higher-level positions may be a result of ignorance of performance or the lack of operational performance standards for high-level officials. Also, it is highly possible that higher-level officials learn to demand deference in most cases because it is due them hierarchically.

According to Thompson, the current concept of bureaucracy is "monistic." Each superior tells his subordinate what to do. Each subordinate is closely supervised by his superior and no one else. Each superior holds his subordinate responsible for performance. Authority within the organization comes down from the top. This concept of the monistic organization is based on the following assumptions. First, it is assumed that the superior is more capable than his subordinates. Second, it is assumed that the superior has the ability and the capacity to determine the results of his unit member. Third, it is assumed that nonhierarchical expertise is not relevant to the operation of the organization.

In the monistic concept, there must be a way to account for specialized activity. This is done by the concept of nonhierarchical authority, an authority created by the delegation of the superior. Thus, the staff specialist may exist, but he can only advise. It is not within the prerogative of the staff members to command. As required skills increase, more nonhierarchical authority is required in an organization. Where nonhierarchical authority exists, the right of appeal exists. This type of authority is more specific than hierarchical authority. It usually has to do with precise functions and activities. It relates or organization goals rather than personal goals. It can usually be appealed by those upon whom it is used. It can be withdrawn without destroying the function. Nonhierarchical authority is organizationally defined.

The existence and emphasis on the monistic formulation causes problems. In earlier organizations, the hierarchical roles were developed when the higher officials were the best at the job. Increasing technology makes it more difficult for those in hierarchical positions to maintain high skill levels. Organizations attempt to retain the hierarchy and fit the specialists to it. The monistic concept cannot, however, account for specialization. The concept of nonhierarchical authority is incompatible with it. The monistic concept causes a split between the right to make a decision and the ability to make it. The emphasis on a monistic concept does not provide for the legitimacy of conflict which does occur in organizations. Therefore, there must be significant effort on the part of those in the organization to smooth over such conflict.

Conflict

Organizations may be viewed as a factoring of broad goals to simpler and more specific sets of activities. This factoring causes the general structure of the organization. It is a function of the technology and instrumental, or goal-directed, considerations. It is determined by specialization. Factoring, along with specialization, results in the creation of nonhierarchical authority. The assignment of work to an individual, and to units, is at least initially an executive function.

The goals for which an organization can strive are technical questions. Thus, they are a function of specialization. Specialists may be viewed as persons skilled in a number of specific programs. However, the superior in the hierarchy has the right to approve organizational goals. The acceptance of innovation is probably based upon the utility of it as judged by the hierarchy in relation to the purposes or values of the organization. Yet innovation is very much a specialist function. The right to change organizational goals is a hierarchical right, but the goal which the organization is able to work toward is a technical, or specialist question.

In large, complex organizations, there is usually a need to involve many specialists, or departments of specialists, in problem-solving. This may be because of instrumental considerations or simply because of a hierarchically created relationship. At any rate, there is an increasing need to rely on specialists as the organization grows. The superior may use this need for the involvement of specialists, or coordination, to increase his power. He may delegate authority in such a manner as to create interdependencies so that he must be called in to settle differences. He is also generally able to define the problem that the group must work on. He may be protected from the influence of the group by his status and prestige, but he may at the same time have a strong influence on the group.

Organizations must also offer the individual the opportunity to satisfy his personal goals beyond the official distribution of power, capacity, and rights. The ability to achieve high levels of job satisfaction may be negatively affected by the definition of hierarchical roles. The elements required for job satisfaction may conflict with the superior's right to assign jobs and supervise them, or they may conflict with the independence of the individual. The fact that the superior can monopolize official communication may be damaging to personal satisfaction. The denial of pertinent information requirements may result in the inability of the subordinate to see the relationship between his activities and group objectives.

As one climbs higher in the organizational hierarchy, opportunity for job satisfaction decreases because of decreasing specialist content in the job. Higher-level officials generally become more oriented toward goals such as power, prestige, and money. As one proceeds up the organizational ladder, adequate operational performance standards decrease. This may result in increased anxiety for those at higher levels, and the incumbent may take some action to solidify his prestige by insisting upon hierarchical rights.

There is perhaps a more significant impact on the personal goal within organizations. The hierarchy in organization has appropriated the concept of success, or achievement of high status. To be successful culturally, one must proceed up a hierarchy. The problem, however, is that the hierarchy is able to manipulate the distributive system in large part. The resulting distribution of organizational rewards and prestige is skewed, and therefore may seem unjust to those who wish to succeed. It may reduce the willingness to cooperate.

There are only a few high-status positions in the hierarchy. Admission may be based on some factors other than relevant performance. The individual most likely to get promoted may be the one who is most like those presently in hierarchical positions. Merit and ability may be overlooked. Some who should achieve success do not, and as a result do not identify with the organization. This may reduce cohesiveness, thereby losing one of the bases of cooperation. This condition essentially denies social recognition and status to many.

Conflict arises from growing inconsistencies between specialists and hierarchical roles. The existence of conflict in an organization is difficult to handle because it is not formally recognized or legitimated within a monistic system. Thus, the existence of specialist-hierarchical role conflict generates the mechanism of role defense. These role defenses are adopted by both specialists and those in hierarchical roles. Specialist role defenses are oriented primarily toward the profession, or the skill area in which the specialist functions or operates. He may seek peer support. The role defense of those in hierarchical positions is somewhat different. Generally they rely on ideology, bureaupathology, and dramaturgy. The remainder of this discussion of Thompson's views emphasizes hierarchical role defense mechanisms.

Ideology

Originally, organizations were headed by charismatic leaders. They were able to exercise authority. Members responded to their attempts to influence them. But growth of specialization has lessened the force of charisma—and made necessary the protection of the hierarchical role in the monistic system. Role definition and authority in bureaucracies must be legitimated. Three defense mechanisms have emerged. These are (1) ideology, (2) dramaturgy, and (0) bureaupathic behavior.

Power is the ability to influence others. If it is legitimate, it is called "authority." Ideas and concepts which justify power held by a person are called "ideology." Where ideology is used, the attention of organization members is usually diverted from the institutional structure. Ideology is used to justify power or authority by attempting to show that those who hold the power are the most qualified to do so, or that the incumbent authority is best for all. Thus, attention is diverted from problems which arise from the organizational structure.

The fact that the force of charisma has declined in the organization has resulted in three general methods to develop ideology. First, leadership studies have been concerned with attempting to determine the traits of leadership. Second, the field of managerial psychology has emerged. This field has attempted to fit people in organizations into existing monistic structures. Problems of intergroup conflict and divergent goals can be solved by training, communications, and reorientation of members. It is assumed that the individual can be changed to fit the structure, hence there is no need to change the present monistic form. Third, the monistic concept, the emphasis on responsibility and authority, is continued. It still holds that "specialists advise and point out the implications of their advice, while the responsibility for implementation belongs to the hierarchy." Since this is not the actual case in organizations, it is necessary to control impressions about hierarchical positions. Such control of impressions is called "dramaturgy."

Dramaturgy

Dramaturgy is the control of information or cues imparted to others to control their impressions. Specialists, as well as those in hierarchical role positions, engage in dramaturgical behavior. The doctor's white coat and the engineer's slide rule suggest the qualifications of each of these specialists. Legitimation in the organization is especially critical because of the specialist-hierarchy gap. The greater the discrepancy, the greater the acting on the part of both members. Organizationally-defined specialties conflict with culturally-defined rights of the hierarchy. Therefore, a staff must only advise. If this advice comes in the form of commands, everyone pretends it is from a higher official. This protects the self-images of those receiving specialist's commands and communications. This is essential for maintaining the legitimacy of hierarchical roles. The impressions that the superior is supposed to convey to his subordinates are that he is industrious, busy, and loyal to the organization. The status system and symbols used in the organization aid in the dramaturgical process. Large offices, deep carpets, and special furniture aid in the creation of the correct impression. The superiors must be somewhat aloof and apart from lower-level members. They must have good records of performance in their job. They must be able to control their emotions, and be careful about behavior and contacts away from work.

Subordinates also engage in dramaturgy. They must be "awed" by their superiors. They must create the impression that they must be told what to do. Subordinates are supposed to look busy.

Bureaupathology

Individuals must adjust to organizations. Those who do, engage in "bureaucratic," or normal behavior. Some individuals, however, are unable to adjust to organizations. This inability to adjust is called "bureausis." Others may be insecure in a bureaucracy. This may result in excessive aloofness, excessive concern with routine and procedures, and resistance to change. This is called "bureaupathology."

Bureaupathology occurs when a superior appropriates the major aspects of the bureaucratic organization for satisfaction of personal needs. It is essentially exercised downward. The superior has a need to control subordinates and to make them conform to a set of preconceived standards.

Organizational success may result in insecurity and anxiety. As one proceeds up organizational levels, performance standards become less objective. The individual knows he must please his boss, but he does not know how. Anxiety may also occur when the position which an individual fills is not accepted by "significant others." The growing gap between the specialist role and the hierarchical role also produces some anxiety. The superior is in a dilemma. He must satisfy nonexplicit performance demands of his superior through subordinates whose skill and abilities he hardly understands. An insecure person may not be able to tolerate this. He may then generate pressures down the line which are passed all through the organization at lower levels. He may emphasize characteristics of the bureaucracy. This has a circular effect. As employees are subjected to greater pressures, they may deviate from the desired standards. As this occurs, the manager's anxiety is increased, and he may begin to insist still more upon the rights and prerogatives of the office he holds.

Bureaupathological behavior may result in quantitative compliance with the standards. That is, individuals may comply with the letter of the law, but not the spirit. Standards applied may be relatively trivial, but there is a need for quantitative measurement since controls can be applied only when standards are available.

Exaggerated aloofness of a superior is also another outcome of bureaupathology. Normal relationships in an organization are not warm in any case, but exaggerated aloofness protects the superiors from commitments to the subordinates so that he can require them to perform when demanded from above.

Another result of pathological behavior in organizations is resistance to change. Innovations are dangerous since they are difficult to control. Risk is involved, which the superior may be unwilling to take in any significant degree. The superior may also insist upon petty rights of office, or protocol. He may engage in close supervision and insist on exclusive contact with outsiders and higher-level officials. Bureaupathological behavior exists because of the growing insecurity of authority and the hierarchical role in organizations. Increasing specialization results in increasing incompatability with the concept of the monistic form of organization. Bureaupathological responses to insecurity are facilitated since there is a routinization of organization problem-solving.

Some people are not able to adjust to bureaucracy. They view it as a curse and a condition which should not exist. Their view of organization is immature. They may engage in "bureautic" behavior. This may be viewed as the dysfunctional persistence of childish behavior patterns. The individual feels powerless in the organization. He attempts to fight the system. He feels that it does not respond to his needs, and that people may be out to "get" him. He resists "red tape" and may view the requirement to respond and comply with his superior as unnecessary.

In summary, then, there are three kinds of behavior patterns in organizations. The first is bureaucratic in nature. These patterns refer to the workings of the large, complex organization, which are determined by the nature of specialization involved. The second is bureaupathology. This involves exaggerations of behavior by insecure persons in hierarchical and nonhierarchical positions. Lastly, bureautic behavior is a reaction to modern organizations by persons who are unable to adjust to the complexity, impersonality, and impartiality of organizations. This type of behavior is viewed as immature.

Cooperation

While management may be outwardly concerned with output, it must also be concerned with the function of obtaining cooperation of members. The methods which it may use are many. It may attempt to command, or rely heavily on a hierarchy, or obtain cooperation by means of group identification. This latter method suggests that the informal group regulates behavior. Thus, it is necessary to get the informal organization working with the formal aspect. Thompson suggests that cooperation may be most easily obtained when it is based on mutually recognized interdependence. Where there is a need to cooperate, this will be recognized. The need will be met. In addition, however, there is still the need for some legitimating devices. These must be held to a minimum. In order to secure cooperation through the recognition of mutual interdependence, it is necessary that there by equality of opportunity and distribution of rewards within the organization.

7 Adaptive Systems Theory

● This chapter focuses on what James D. Thompson (34) has called the "natural system" approach, which is concerned with the organization as a unit in interaction with its environment. In this approach, the organization is considered as a complex set of interdependent parts interacting with one another and dependent in whole or some larger environment. Organizational survival is the goal and the organization will adapt in such a way as to achieve it. Thompson notes that "dysfunctions are conceivable, but it is assumed that the offending part will adjust to produce a net positive contribution or be disengaged or else this system will degenerate." Thompson does not, however, as others have done, dismiss the other strategies of organization analysis, that is, the closed system methods. He suggests that both these approaches lead to some "truth, but neither alone affords an adequate understanding of complex organization."

The first selection, a summary/review of Selznick's work, is consistent with this natural system point of view. Selznick focuses on external organizations and how they may be fundamentally important in defining the nature of the organization. Cooptation is an adjustment process which facilitates the probabilities of survival of the organization. Cooptation is a mechanism used when the structure of the organization is inconsistent with the external environment imposing pressures on it. It is the process of absorbing new elements into leadership or policy-determination positions.

Selznick also points to the unanticipated consequences of individual activities in an organization. Some have suggested that the classical theorists presuppose away the notions of conflict and dysfunction by designing organization structure rigidly. While this may have been done in theory, it is impossible to do in fact. Selznick highlights the problems that could occur.

Selznick, however, does not describe alternative organization forms that might be appropriate in various types of environment. He simply describes the need for adaptation and some mechanisms by which it might occur. Burns and Stalker provide important insights into alternative organization forms. While there have been a number of critics of classical theory and the theory of bureaucracy, the major alternative form proposed by most tends to approximate a democratic organization. Yet when this organization form is put against the realities of the world, it is as ill-fitting as bureaucracy in many instances. Burns and Stalker suggest that the important variable to be considered is the environment. Essentially, they believe that in a relatively stable situation, a mechanistic (or bureaucratic) structure may be substantially more effective than one which approaches a democratic ideal. In a highly variable, or volatile environment, however, more flexible forms, which they call "organic," would be appropriate.

Borrowing from Burns and Stalker, and in an attempt to increase the understanding of organizational/effectiveness relationships, Joan Woodward and her associates undertook a research project which may well mark a turning point in the development of theory about organizations. An empirically-based work that examined a large sample of British firms, her study provides strong evidence for the intuitive criticisms that there is no *one* best way to organize. Woodward's work points sharply to some prescriptions that might be useful to the practitioner.

Further theoretical development of these notions is provided in James Thompson's approach. Thompson is especially concerned with the lack of "good" theory for use by researchers. He attempts an integration of concepts from a wide range of social science literature to deal with the important questions of how organizations adapt to and cope with the environment.

Perrow, in the last selection in this chapter, presents detail not developed elsewhere. IIis formulation includes the extreme ends of the organization spectrum, but he also describes "mixed" forms and some attendant problems for participants in them. His concept of variability of particular environmental sectors, and the way this is linked to structure, is important, for it makes abundantly clear that structure decisions may not be at the discretion of individuals inside the organization.—H.L.T.

Selznick's "TVA and the Grass Roots"

HENRY L. TOSI

Selznick's basic aim in *TVA and the Grass Roots* is to present an approach to analyzing organizations. He is concerned with behavior that is internally relevant to them, and attempts to examine structural conditions which influence that behavior.

The organization is an adaptive social structure. It is a technical instrument for mobilizing human energies and directing them toward set aims. It is a mechanism which adapts to its environment. It is molded by forces tangential to its rational, ordered structure and stated goals. The

Summarized from Philip Selznick, *TVA and the Grass Roots* (Berkeley: University of California Press, 1953). I assume full responsibility for the interpretation herein.

organization may be viewed as a dynamic conditioning field which shapes the behavior of those at its helm (and implicity other members). It is a tool which has a life of its own separate from that of the members, yet mobilizing interacting humans to get the work done. Organizations are living social units which must come to terms with the environment. Organization behavior can best be understood when it is traced to the needs and structure of the organization as a living social institution.

Organizations have certain needs generated by the organization itself which command the attention and the decisions of those in power. In order to satisfy these needs, the organization must be adaptive to the environment in which it operates. These needs are:

1) the security of the organization in the social environment—this requires some continuity of policy and leadership;

2) maintenance of the stability of lines of communication and authority;

3) a homogeneous outlook of participants regarding the meaning and role of the organization;

4) the achievement of continuous support and participation on the part of the members; and

5) the stability of informal relations within the organization.

The formal and informal structure of activities within the organization develops in response to these needs. The organization can continue to exist only when it satisfies these needs and comes to terms with the environment. An informal structure develops within the formal structure of the organization. This informal structure reflects attempts of individuals and subgroups to control the conditions of their existence. It contains an informal control and communications mechanism, or system. This informal structure may be useful to the formal leadership as a communication device, but it extracts a cost for its existence: some power is taken from the formal system.

External organizations

The characteristics of the organization may be determined by the constraints of other organizations in the environment. External organizations or groups sometimes have a special relationship to the organization. This may require that both the organization and the external body support each other in some way. The organization may have some responsibility to the external units, such as clients, customers, or the public. The character of this external group tends to define and shape the character of the organization. Somehow, it must be represented. It may be formally represented. The organization may recruit external unit members as organization members. They may also absorb them into the leadership structure of the organization. When the outside organization is not formally represented, it must rely on the ideology (to be discussed later) or some other mechanism to maintain the relationship. These external relationships affect the character and policy of the organization since adjustment to them is required.

Cooptation

One way that the organization comes to terms with the environment is through the mechanism of cooptation. Cooptation is an adjustment, or coping, mechanism which enhances the chances of survival of the organization. It is needed when formal authority is out of balance with the institutional environment. It is the process of absorbing new elements into the leadership or policy-determining structure of the organization as a means of averting threats to the organization's stability and existence. It is an attempt to accommodate to the existing environment. In effect, power is shared with other interested groups.

Cooptation may be viewed in both formal and informal dimensions. Formal cooptation occurs when those absorbed into the policy-making and leadership structure share in the power as well as the burdens of administration. This happens when the organization publicly absorbs new elements. It is required when it is necessary to enhance or increase the legitimacy of the governing group, or where there is need for self-government within the organization.

Cooptation may be, however, a response to specific power centers. Informal cooptation is an internal response to the specific pressures of power within the community or the organization. In this case, the coopted elements share only in the power. It is an internal adaptation of the system when the formal authority structure is threatened. The power nucleus of affected groups may be absorbed into the organization to appease or reduce the opposition of other groups. Informal cooptation is a recognition of and a concession to the human resources in the organization. This type of cooptation may *not* be formally acknowledged.

Cooptation reflects the existing tension between social power and formal authority. When formal authority and social power exist together, there is no need for it. Cooptation broadens the leadership and has an important effect on the governing body. It restricts alternatives available to them. There is a need to accommodate the organization to those who have been coopted.

Cooptation is, in fact, a form of delegation. Those who coopt (the leaders) must be concerned with objectives and the means for achieving them. But they must also be concerned with those whom the organization affects. When either formal or informal cooptation occurs, the organization commits itself to activities supported and reinforced by the coopted elements. Thus, it must reach an equilibrium with those coopted, the objectives, the means of achieving them, and the environment. Thus cooptation, even though relatively slight, exerts pressure throughout the organization.

As a result of cooptation, a flow of information may be provided to those who have been coopted. Additionally, the organization is provided with the group resources of those coopted members. Cooptation also allows adaptation of decisions to lower, or local, levels of the organization. Therefore, other organizations within the environment which have been coopted shape the characteristics and the nature of the coopting organization.

Ideology

Organizations are like people, searching for stability and meaning. Instability in the environment results in the development of a sustaining ideology, especially when the organization is threatened by the surrounding environment. It is necessary that this ideology be based on accepted political and moral values. The organization ideology serves as a parameter for decisions.

Ideology, or doctrine, arises as a special need of the organization. The source of ideology in the organization may be (1) from the influence of other institutions, and/or (2) the result of the need for internal communications to develop stability and homogeneity of attitudes.

Ideology facilitates the decentralization of management to lower levels. It shapes the views of how members as well as uniting technical experts within the bounds of the organization rather than toward their professions. Ideology may also emerge as organization members defend it against outsiders. Thus, doctrine, or ideology, satisfies internal needs but also provides an adjustment mechanism for the organization through which it can interact with other segments of the environment. It does not, however, provide a complete adjustment mechanism.

Ideology most probably is stated in language which is ambiguous to the members. The meanings of concepts included in it may be different for different members. For instance, the concept of "increased effectiveness" might suggest reduced operating costs to a production foreman, while it may mean a more restrictive quality control policy to the quality-control staff executive. These ambiguities, however, mean something to members in terms of the specific activity in which they engage. The diverse meanings of ideology begin to take shape and become concrete through administrative decisions. Decisions must be made within discretionary bounds of the executive. Discretion has to do with the selection of alternatives. When it is used it involves, in some cases, intervention in the activities of other people. It is necessary therefore to consider the interests of those whom the decisions affect.

Decisions must be made within "ideology." The existence and use of abstract philosophies and ideologies to control organization result in problems. Ideology is abstract and action is specific. The resolution of this dilemma is ongoing activity. Specific action programs must be developed to achieve these abstractions. The activities generally required to achieve abstractions may in practice be difficult to implement. Additionally, the delegation process separates planning functions (which may be derived from the philosophy or ideology) from the operating or specific activity.

Decisions made within the discretion bounds are inhibited by pressure groups within and outside the organization. Some policies may be highly dependent upon the connection the organization has with external organizations. For instance, the return goods policy of industrial manufacturers may be a function of "real control" that the buyer has over the seller.

Unanticipated consequences

Lower-level officials of the organization must make decisions. In some cases, when there is ambiguity regarding the job content of these lower-level officials, their decisions may be based on their own values and norms. These may be inconsistent with, or different from, those of others in the organization. They may also be inconsistent or different from the objectives of the organization. Policy and doctrine attempt to generate action which is intended to be rational. Decisions within the discretion boundaries of administrators, however, require that they act selectively within their environment, which is conditioned by their own interests, values, or internalized norms. These decisions may yield results other than those intended within the concept of the ideology.

There are several reasons why these unanticipated consequences may occur. First, the individual may have commitments to other places or other organizational units which exert pressures contrary to the ideology. The external commitments of groups or members, (basic values, norms, and loyalties) may result in the inability of that organizational component to adjust to other aspects of the organization and to the organization's structure. This is most likely when these various commitments and norms are divergent.

Decisions made by higher-level organization members may commit lower levels to specific actions which the lower levels may not deem desirable. The interests of subgroups or departments must be viewed in light of the social situations within which their activities are carried on and the long-run consequences to the organization. Some activities necessary to maintain the organization may have, then, undesirable consequences for subordinate units. Some acts are simply required, such as procedures, which may become ends in themselves to these lower-level units. When this happens the unit may become more concerned with the performance of the function rather than the end which is desired as a result of performance. This preoccupation with means rather than ends may be harmful to the organization, yet these commitments may be enforced by the social environment and institutionalization.

The individual's personality also must be considered in obtaining unanticipated results. His needs, personal history, and experiences may result in a personality which rejects the demands of others, yet he must conform to some degree. Resistance to change and conflict may develop.

The organization strives, however, for a unified pattern of responses. This requires unity, or homogeneity, of outlook of members. As unity is approximated, the organizational character emerges. This may be essentially described as the way people live together in an organization. Those who cannot tolerate this character leave the organization.

The discretion of an executive is related to the organization character in the following manner. By increasing and integrating the many responses within an organization, it can be invested with a character. Precedent and custom then tend to preserve this character. When organizational conflict exists, the process of decisions, or the use of discretion, will be closely scrutinized. The administrator's decision will be infused with a high degree of self-consciousness.

The internal pressures toward unity are generated by the interests, values, and ideas which characterize the social environment of the organization. Once the organization has selected from the many alternative philosophies and values available, the organization reflects on its own character and sentiment to which it becomes aligned. These philosophies and values are available in the social environment, or context, within which the organization operates.

Additionally, different philosophies and values may be representative of various groups within the organization. This may be an unanticipated result of cooptation of members with divergent views. As each group attempts to make its basic philosophy predominant, a struggle for influence may ensue. The internal struggle between these groups is important in the concept of organizational leadership. The struggle results in the evolution of "organizational character." This means that if the organization character changes, the leadership which stands for those ideals may be placed in a power position. Or leadership may change the character of the organization by gaining unity of thought regarding a particular ideology.

Another paradox for leadership in an organization should be considered. Leadership, by its nature, is involved with conflicting goals and problems. If it ignores the participation of the members, then the cooperation level may be threatened. If it encourages participation, however, its leadership position may be threatened by the acceptance of another ideology by other organization members.

The Management of Innovation

T. BURNS AND G. M. STALKER

. . . The utility of the notions of "mechanistic" and "organic" management systems resides largely in their being related as dependent variables to the rate of "environmental" change. "Environmental," in this connection, refers to the technological basis of production and to the market situation . . . . The increasing rate of technological change characteristic of the last generation could plausibly be regarded as a function of fundamental changes in the relationship of production to consumption.

If the form of management is properly to be seen as dependent on the situation the concern is trying to meet, it follows that there is no single set of principles for "good organization," an ideal type of management system which can serve as a model to which administrative practice should, or could in time, approximate. It follows also that there is an overriding

Excerpted with permission of the publisher from T. Burns and G. M. Stalker, *The Management of Innovation* (London: Tavistock Publications, 1961).

management task in first interpreting correctly the market and technological situation, in terms of its instability or of the rate at which conditions are changing, and then designing the management system appropriate to the conditions, and making it work. "Direction," as I have labelled this activity, is the distinctive task of managers-in-chief. . . .

For the individual, much of the importance of the difference between mechanistic and organic systems lies in the extent of his commitment to the working organization. Mechanistic systems (namely 'bureaucracies') define his functions, together with the methods, responsibilities, and powers appropriate to them; in other words, however, this means that boundaries are set. That is to say, in being told what he has to attend to, and how, he is also told what he does not have to bother with, what is not his affair, what is not expected of him, what he can post elsewhere as the responsibility of others. In organic systems, the boundaries of feasible demands on the individual disappear. The greatest stress is placed on his regarding himself as fully implicated in the discharge of any task appearing over his horizon, as involved not merely in the exercise of a special competence but in commitment to the success of the concern's undertakings approximating somewhat to that of the doctor or scientist in the discharge of his professional functions. . .

Mechanistic and organic systems

We are now at the point at which we may set down the outline of the two management systems which represent for us . . . the two polar extremities of the forms which such systems can take when they are adapted to a specific rate of technical and commercial change. The case we have tried to establish from the literature, as from our research experience . . . , is that the different forms assumed by a working organization do exist objectively and are not merely interpretations offered by observers of different schools.

Both types represent a "rational" form of organization, in that they may both, in our experience, be explicitly and deliberately created and maintained to exploit the human resources of a concern in the most efficient manner feasible in the circumstances of the concern. Not surprisingly, however, each exhibits characteristics which have been hitherto associated with different kinds of interpretation. For it is our contention that empirical findings have usually been classified according to sociological ideology rather than according to the functional specificity of the working organization to its task and the conditions confronting it.

We have tried to argue that these are two formally contrasted forms of management system. These we shall call the mechanistic and organic form.

A *mechanistic* management system is appropriate to stable conditions. It is characterized by:

(a) the specialized differentiation of functional tasks into which the problems and tasks facing the concern as a whole are broken down;

(b) the abstract nature of each individual task, which is pursued with techniques and purposes more or less distinct from those of the concern as a whole; i.e., the functionaries tend to pursue the technical improvement of means, rather than the accomplishment of the ends of the concern;

(c) the reconciliation, for each level in the hierarchy, of these distinct performances by the immediate superiors, who are also, in turn, responsible for seeing that each is relevant in his own special part of the task.

(d) the precise definition of rights and obligations and technical methods attached to each functional role;

(e) the translation of rights and obligations and methods into the responsibilities of a functional position;

(f) hierarchic structure of control, authority and communication;

(g) a reinforcement of the hierarchic structure by the location of knowledge of actualities exclusively at the top of the hierarchy, where the final reconciliation of distinct tasks and assessment of relevance is made.[1]

(h) a tendency for interaction between members of the concern to be vertical, i.e., between superior and subordinate;

(i) a tendency for operations and working behavior to be governed by the instructions and decisions issued by superiors;

(j) insistence on loyalty to the concern and obedience to superiors as a condition of membership;

(k) a greater importance and prestige attaching to internal (local) than to general (cosmopolitan) knowledge, experience, and skill.

The *organic* form is appropriate to changing conditions, which give rise constantly to fresh problems and unforeseen requirements for action which cannot be broken down or distributed automatically arising from the functional roles defined within a hierarchic structure. It is characterized by:

(a) the contributive nature of special knowledge and experience to the common task of the concern;

(b) the "realistic" nature of the individual task, which is seen as set by the total situation of the concern;

(c) the adjustment and continual re-definition of individual tasks through interaction with others;

(d) the shedding of "responsibility" as a limited field of rights, obligations and methods. (Problems may not be posted upwards, downwards or sideways as being someone else's responsibility);

(e) the spread of commitment to concern beyond any technical definition;

(f) a network structure of control, authority, and communication. The sanctions which apply to the individual's conduct in his working role derive more from presumed community of interest with the rest of the working organization in the survival and growth of the firm, and less from a contractual relationship between himself and a non-personal corporation, represented for him by an immediate superior;

(g) omniscience no longer imputed to the head of the concern; knowledge about the technical or commercial nature of the here and now task may be located anywhere in the network; this location becoming the *ad hoc* center of control authority and communication.

(h) a lateral rather than a vertical direction of communication through the organization, communication between people of different rank, also, resembling consultation rather than command;

(i) a content of communication which consists of information and advice rather than instructions and decisions;

(j) commitment to the concern's tasks and to the "technological ethos" of material progress and expansion is more highly valued than loyalty and obedience;

(k) importance and prestige attach to affiliations and expertise valid in the industrial and technical and commercial milieux external to the firm.

One important corollary to be attached to this account is that while organic systems are not hierarchic in the same sense as are mechanistic, they remain stratified. Positions are differentiated according to seniority—i.e., greater expertise. The lead in joint decisions is frequently taken by seniors, but it is an essential presumption of the organic system that the lead, i.e., "authority," is taken by whoever shows himself most informed and capable, i.e., the "best authority." The location of authority is settled by consensus.

A second observation is that the area of commitment to the concern—the extent to which the individual yields himself as a resource to be used by the working organization—is far more extensive in organic than in mechanistic systems. Commitment, in fact, is expected to approach that of the professional scientist to his work, and frequently does. One further consequence of this is that it becomes far less feasible to distinguish "informal" from "formal" organization.

Thirdly, the emptying out of significance from the hierarchic command system, by which co-operation is ensured and which serves to monitor the working organization under a mechanistic system, is encountered by the development of shared beliefs about the values and goals of the concern. The growth and accretion of institutionalized values, beliefs, and conduct, in the forms of commitments, ideology, and manners, around an image of the concern in its industrial and commercial setting make good the loss of formal structure.

Finally, the two forms of system represent a polarity, not a dichotomy; there are . . . intermediate stages between the extremities empirically known to us. Also, the relation of one form to the other is elastic, so that a concern oscillating between relative stability and relative change may also oscillate between the two forms. A concern may (and frequently does) operate with a management system which includes both types.

The organic form, by departing from the familiar clarity and fixity of the hierarchic structure, is often experienced by the individual manager as an uneasy, embarrassed, or chronically anxious quest for knowledge about what he should be doing, or what is expected of him, and similar apprehensiveness about what others are doing. Indeed, as we shall see later, this kind of response is necessary if the organic form of organization is to work effectively. Understandably, such anxiety finds expression in resentment when the apparent confusion besetting him is not explained. In these situations, all managers some of the time, and many managers all the time, yearn for more definition and structure.

On the other hand, some managers recognize a rationale of nondefinition, a reasoned basis for the practice of those successful firms in which designation of status, function, and line of responsibility and authority has been vague or even avoided.

The desire for more definition is often in effect a wish to have the limits of one's task more neatly defined—to know what and when one doesn't have to bother about as much as to know what one does have to. It follows that the more definition is given, the more omniscient the management must be, so that no functions are left wholly or partly undischarged, no person is. overburdened with undelegated responsibility, or left without the authority to do his job properly. To do this, to have all the separate functions attached to individual roles fitting together and comprehensively, to have communication between persons constantly maintained on a level adequate to the needs of each functional role, requires rules or traditions of behavior proved over a long time and an equally fixed, stable task. The omniscience which may then be credited to the head of the concern is expressed throughout its body through the lines of command, extending in a clear, explicitly titled hierarchy of officers and subordinates.

The whole mechanistic form is instinct with this twofold principle of definition and dependence which acts as the frame within which action is conceived and carried out. It works, unconsciously, almost in the smalloot minutiae of daily activity. "How late is late?" The answer to this question is not to bo found in the rule book, but in the superior. Late is when the boss thinks it is late. Is he the kind of man who thinks 8:00 is the time, and 8:01 is late? Does he think that 8:15 is all right occasionally if it is not a regular thing? Does he think that everyone should be allowed a 5-minutes grace after 8:00 but after that they are late?

Settling questions about how a person's job is to be done in this way is nevertheless simple, direct, and economical of effort. . . .

One other feature of mechanistic organization needs emphasis. It is a necessary condition of its operation that the individual "works on his own," functionally isolated; he "knows his job," he is "responsible for seeing it's done." He works at a job which is in a sense artificially abstracted from the realities of the situation the concern is dealing with, the accountant "dealing with the costs side," the works manager "pushing production," and so on. As this works out in practice, the rest of the organization becomes part of the problem situation the individual has to deal with in order to perform successfully; i.e., difficulties and problems arising from work or information which has been handed over the "responsibility barrier" between two jobs or departments are regarded as "really" the responsibility of the person from whom they were received. As a design engineer put in, "When you get designers handing over designs completely to production, it's their responsibility now. And you get tennis games played with the responsibility for anything that goes wrong. What happens is that you're constantly getting unsuspected faults arising from characteristics which you didn't think important in the design. If you get to hear of these through a sales person, or a production person, or somebody to whom the design was handed over to in the dim past, then, instead of being a design problem, it's an annoyance caused by that particular person, who can't do his own, job—because you'd thought you were finished with that one, and you're on to something else now."

When the assumptions of the form of organization make for preoccupation with specialized tasks, the chances of career success, or of greater influence, depend rather on the relative importance which may be attached to each special function by the superior whose task it is to reconcile and control a number of them. And, indeed, to press the claims of one's job or department for a bigger share of the firm's resources is in many cases regarded as a mark of initiative, of effectiveness, and even of "loyalty to the firm's interests." The state of affairs thus engendered squares with the role of the superior, the man who can see the wood instead of just the trees, and gives it the reinforcement of the aloof detachment belonging to a court of appeal. The ordinary relationship prevailing between individual managers "in charge of" different functions is one of rivalry, a rivalry which may be rendered innocuous to the persons involved by personal friendship or the norms of sociability, but which turns discussion about the situations which constitute the real problems of the concern—how to make products more cheaply, how to sell more, how to allocate resources, whether to curtail activity in one sector, whether to risk expansion in another, and so on—into an arena of conflicting interests.

The distinctive feature of the second, organic system is the pervasiveness of the working organization as an institution. In concrete terms, this makes itself felt in a preparedness to combine with others in serving the general aims of the concern. Proportionately to the rate and extent of change, the less can the omniscience appropriate to command organizations be ascribed to the head of the organization; for executives, and even operatives, in a changing firm it is always theirs to reason why. Furthermore, the less definition can be given to status, roles, and modes of communication, the more do the activities of each member of the organization become determined by the real tasks of the firm as he sees them than by instruction and routine. The individual's job ceases to be self-contained; the only way in which "his" job can be done is by his participating continually with others in the solution of problems which are real to the firm, and put in a language of requirements and activities meaningful to them all. Such methods of working put much heavier demands on the individual. . . .

We have endeavored to stress the appropriateness of each system to its own specific set of conditions. Equally, we desire to avoid the suggestion that either system is superior under all circumstances to the other. In particular, nothing in our experience justifies the assumption that mechanistic systems should be superseded by organic in conditions of stability.[2] The beginning of administrative wisdom is the awareness that there is no optimum type of management system.

Footnotes

[1] This functional attribute of the head of a concern often takes on a clearly expressive aspect. It is common enough for concerns to instruct all people with whom they deal to address correspondence to the firm (i.e., to its formal head) and for all outgoing letters and orders to be signed by the head of the concern. Similarly, the printed letter heading used by Government departments carries instructions for the replies to be addressed to the Secretary, etc. These instructions are not always taken seriously, either by members of the organization or their correspondents, but in one company this practice was insisted upon and was taken to somewhat unusual lengths; *all* correspondence was delivered to the managing director, who would thereafter distribute excerpts to members of the staff, synthesizing their replies into the

letter of reply which he eventually sent. Telephone communication was also controlled by limiting the numbers of extensions, and by monitoring incoming and outgoing calls.

2 [An] instance of this assumption is contained in H. A. Shepard's paper addressed to the Symposium on the Direction of Research Establishments, 1956: "There is much evidence to suggest that the optimal use of human resources in industrial organizations requires a different set of conditions, assumptions, and skills from those traditionally present in industry. Over the past twenty-five years, some new orientations have emerged from organizational experiments, observations and inventions. The new orientations depart radically from doctrines associated with 'Scientific Management' and traditional bureaucratic patterns.

"The central emphases in this development are as follows:

"1. Wide participation in decision-making, rather than centralized decision-making.

"2. The face-to-face group, rather than the individual, as the basic unit of organization.

"3. Mutual confidence, rather than authority, as the integrative force in organization.

"4. The supervisor as the agent for maintaining intragroup and intergroup communication, rather than as the agent of higher authority.

"5. Growth of members of the organization to greater responsibility, rather than external control of the member's performance or their tasks."

Woodward's "Industrial Organization"

DONNA G. GOEHLE

Joan Woodward's book, *Industrial Organization* (38) represents the results of nearly a decade of empirical study of British industry located in South Essex. The research was undertaken by the Human Relations Research Unit at the South East Essex College of Technology beginning in 1953, with the major part of the field work completed in 1958. Additional research, utilizing selected firms and aimed toward in-depth analysis of preliminary findings, was begun in 1960.

The general objective of the research workers in initially approaching the study was that, "a project had to be devised, which, although problem-centered, might make a contribution to the field of industrial sociology." According to Woodward, preliminary findings indicated that in the "final formulation of the project industrial firms would have to be studied as complex social systems and line-staff relationships looked at as parts of a whole rather than in isolation." Moreover, the wide differences between firms indicated that it would be necessary to include as many of the nearby firms as possible; however, such a broadening of the effort brought about additional possibilities for superficial results, and therefore it was decided that the project should first concentrate on making a broad survey of the whole area, and then additional in-depth studies could be undertaken if there were sufficient time and resources made available. Woodward's text presents an account of the studies themselves and the conclusions drawn from an analysis of the data.

The survey and initial conclusions

In the first study of 100 industrial firms conducted between September 1954 and September 1955, the researchers attempted to obtain information regarding the formal organization and operating procedures. It was felt that the large number of firms involved in the first phase of the study would preclude attempts to find out very much about the informal social relationships within the firm; therefore, the information sought by the research unit was limited to the following categories:

1) history, background, and objectives;

2) description of the manufacturing processes and methods;

3) forms and routines through which the firm was organized and operated;

4) facts and figures that could be used to make an assessment of the firm's commercial success.

In evaluating the information regarding history, background and objectives, it became evident that although all firms were engaged in manufacturing, there were substantial differences among them. "The nature of their markets, the type of customers they served, the methods they employed, and the targets they set for themselves differed considerably." The differences in manufacturing processes were also noticeable and were grouped according to the following "technical variables": "the density of production, the flexibility of production, facilities, the diversity of products, the time span of operations, and the way in which production programs were initiated and controlled." (This classification of technical variables related to production types becomes a critical element throughout the entire period of the study.)

In reference to the third category of information sought, the research workers obtained organization charts where they were available, and tried to construct them through interviewing when they were not. Information in this category focused on determining the pattern of prescribed relationships as well as a duties and responsibilities of each office studied. In addition, they studied "the history and responsibilities of the principal staff and specialist departments, including sales, research, development, personnel, inspection, maintenance, and purchasing; they examined the documentation associated with planning and control procedures and the methods used in costing and budgetary control." Considerable attention was also given to analyzing the labor structure for each firm.

Since the researchers were not only interested in determining how the various firms were organized and operated, but also in discovering whether particular forms of organization were associated with managerial efficiency and success, they also attempted to assemble information regarding the ways in which a firm's success might be evaluated internally and externally. Some of the factors taken into account in assessing the "success" of the enterprise included such things as market position and market share, annual reports and financial statements for a five-year period, fluctuations in the market price of the firm's stock, reputation among competitors and labor unions, and internally generated information thought to be significant in explaining the relationship between internal operations and enterprise success.

In developing a measure of commercial success which could be used in testing the relationship between organizational form and that success, the methods used by the researchers seem to be imprecise and are not treated as rigorously as some of the other variables utilized. Internal efficiency, although mentioned, does not appear to be fully developed in either of the studies; however, some oblique references to the efficiency of certain production technologies does appear in the analysis of both studies. Aside from grouping the firms on the basis of the general categories of "average," "above average," and "below average," the researchers did not concentrate their analysis on linking more specific measures of commercial success to particular organizational forms.

In their analysis of organization, Woodward and her colleagues focused primarily on the types of organization traditionally associated with the "classical" school of organizational thought: line organization, functional organization, and line-staff organization. They divided the firms into these categories and found the following distribution of types among the firms surveyed: 35 predominately line organization; 2 functional organization; 59 line-staff organization; and 4 unclassifiable.

A considerable degree of variation, especially in the manner in which specialist departments evolved, existed among the firms surveyed; however, there seemed to be no consistent pattern of evolution which held true across the sample. In addition, firms rated at both ends of the success continuum illustrated diverse organizational forms. According to the study, there did not appear to be a direct interrelationship between organizational structure and commercial success. When other variables were examined, such as the length of the command hierarchy, the sizes of the span of control at various levels, the size of the firm based on total employees, the industry type, and managerial qualifications, no link between one or more variables and commercial success could be established.

Woodward and her associates also utilized Burns' approach to classifying industrial organizations as "mechanistic" and "organic" systems. Applying this classification to the firms being studied, they found that "Organic systems, both those consciously planned on organic lines and those planned on mechanistic lines but operated on organic principles, outnumbered mechanistic systems by approximately two to one." The results of the analysis of the participating firms based on the criteria Burns' work suggested, seem to substantiate his earlier findings. Woodward reports the results in the following manner:

> As a result of his researches he came to the conclusion that mechanistic systems are appropriate to stable conditions and organic systems to conditions of change. It will be recalled that South Essex is an area in which the newer and developing industries predominate, and it might therefore be expected that organic systems would predominate (p. 24).

Having reached these general conclusions in their initial analysis of the data, the researchers turned to a more detailed examination of the technical variables. Although some social scientists, including Weber and Veblen, have suggested a link between technological circumstances and the structure and behavior of social systems, there had been relatively little empirical work undertaken which would delineate this suggested relationship. In the absence of such a framework, Woodward's researchers initially grouped the firms on the basis of similarities in manufacturing processes and methods. Once the initial classification was complete, they were able to determine that "firms with similar goals and associated manufacturing policies had similar manufacturing processes—the range of tools, instruments, machines and technical formulas was limited and controlled by the manufacturing policy." The first breakdown of firms studied included those enterprises "where production was 'one of a kind' to meet customers' individual requirements, and those where production was standardized."

This initial breakdown quickly developed into many more categories based on the size of the unit being produced, the technical complexity of the product being produced, and the diversity of products being manufactured, to mention only a few. It became obvious to the researchers that each of the manufacturing processes was unique in some way; therefore, some method of systematizing the firms according to technical variables had to be developed. "It was felt that the system of division normally used by production engineers into the three categories of jobbing, batch, and mass production were inadequate...." Consequently, a more expanded grouping of eleven categories, based on these three basic production types, was devised. Figure 1 represents the distribution of firms by production system.

In relating the production categories to the ways in which the various firms were organized and operated, the first significant pattern emerged. It was determined that, "firms with similar production systems appeared to have similar organizational structures." According to Woodward, the differences between some of the firms placed in the same category were not as significant as the differences observed between the various categories. Furthermore, "the figures relating to the various organizational characteristics tended to cluster around the medians, the medians varying from one category to another." Based on these observations, the following conclusions were drawn:

> Therefore, the main conclusion reached through this research project was that the existence of the link between technology and social structure first postulated by Thorstein Veblen (1919) can be demonstrated empirically (p. 50).

Although Woodward is careful to note that the research did not prove technology was the *only* important variable in determining the organizational structure, it was one which could be isolated for further study without too much difficulty. In addition, "the only variable found to be demonstrably related to variations in organization was the system of production in operation." In examining this relationship, the following characteristics were also considered: "the length of the line of command; the span of control of the chief executive; the percentage of total turnover allocated to the payment of wages and salaries; and the ratio of managers to total personnel, of clerical and administrative staff to manual workers, of direct to indirect labor, and of graduate to non-graduate supervision in the production departments."

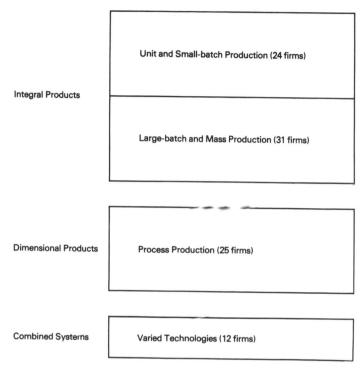

**Figure 1. Production Systems
of Firms in the Study (adapted
from Joan Woodward)**

Throughout this phase of the report, Woodward distinguishes the predominant characteristics of firms operating at both ends of the production continuum as well as in the middle ranges and relates them in a systematic fashion to the variables. She then continues by developing a discussion of the relationship between technology, organization, and success. Since one of the objectives in conducting the study was to determine whether or not management principles were being applied in practice and whether they were influential in ensuring business success, the researchers wanted to determine what type of organizational system might prove to be most appropriate for a particular production system. On the basis of analyzing the preceding organizational characteristics—number of levels in the chain of command, labor costs, and various labor ratios—with measures of organizational success, Woodward concludes that:

> The fact that organizational characteristics, technology and success were linked together in this way suggested that not only was the system of production an important variable in the determination of

organizational structure, but also that one particular form of organization was most appropriate to each system of production. In unit production, for example, not only did short and relatively broadly based pyramids predominate, but they also appeared to ensure success. Process production, on the other hand, would seem to require the taller and more narrowly based pyramid. (p. 71).

Woodward also found that "successful firms inside the large batch production range tended to have mechanistic management systems. On the other hand, successful firms outside this range tended to have organic systems."

In explaining the observations of the Woodward team and their relationship to the concepts associated with classical management theory, she makes the following statement:

> In general, the administrative expedients associated with success in large-batch firms were in line with the principles and ideas on which the teaching of management subjects is based. In all successful large-batch production firms there was not only a clear definition of duties and responsibilities of the kind already referred to, but also an adherence to the principles of unity of command; a separation (at least on paper) of advisory from executive responsibilities, and a chief executive who controlled no more than the recommended five or six direct subordinates.
>
> The tendency to regard large-batch production as the typical system of modern industry may be the explanation of this link between success and conformity with management theory. The people responsible for developing management theory no doubt had large batch production in mind as they speculated about management. In general, the experience on which their generalizations were based had been obtained in large-batch production industry (pp. 71-72).

In summarizing the results of the survey, Woodward states that "While at first sight there seemed to be no link between organization and success, and no one best way or organizing a factory, it subsequently became apparent that there was a particular form of organization most appropriate to each technical situation." According to the survey, "within a limited range of technology this was also the form of organization most closely in line with the principles and ideas of management theory. . . . Outside this limited range however, the rules appear to be different, the most suitable form of organization being out of line with these ideas." It should be noted that Woodward carefully states that the researchers found a link between organization, technology, and success, but that a *precisely defined causal* relationship was not claimed nor established by this phase of the research.

Examining the link between organization and technology, the researchers were also interested in evaluating the relationship between technology, social structure, and administrative practices in general. Viewing the firm as a social system within a larger social system, Woodward defines social structure as the "framework on which the system operates." According to Woodward, the variables in the system include: "occupational structure, the enterprise consisting of members of different occupational groups in the community; formal organization, i.e., the stable and explicit pattern of prescribed relationships designed to enable those employed to work together in the achievement of objectives, and informal organization, i.e., the pattern of relationships which actually emerges from day to day operations." Since the researchers were interested in determining to what degree management theory, as it was being taught, was being applied in designing and administering organizations, it was natural that the analysis would probably move in the direction of further defining the link between technology and organization.

From the information obtained in the survey, Woodward and her colleagues determined that formal organization was considerably affected by technical factors. Although they found that there was less conscious planning of formal organizations in the firms they studied than one would expect, given the findings of several other social scientists in the industrial field, they did discover that some interesting relationships between formal planning of organizational structure, formalization of the informal structure, and the type of production being employed in the enterprise. In the successful firms of the first group (utilizing formal organizational planning), "unit and small-batch production and continuous-flow production predominated, while the majority of successful firms in the second category were in the large-batch production category." This finding would tend to suggest that "conscious planning produces better results in some kinds of industry than in others."

Since other social scientists have frequently assumed that "formal organization is the part of social structure least affected by technology," the conclusions drawn by Woodward seem especially interesting: "the survey findings suggested that the link between technology and organization persists in spite of, rather than because of, the conscious behavior or deliberate policy, and in defiance of the tendency in management education to emphasize the independence of the administrative process from technical considerations." Through her analysis of these findings, she suggests that technical environments can and do affect the structure of both the formal and the informal organization of the enterprise. Furthermore, she contends that "technology, because it influences the roles defined by formal organization, must therefore influence industrial behavior, for how a person reacts depends as much on the demands of his role and the circumstances in which he finds himself, as on his personality." Woodward goes on to state that "there can be occasions when the behavior forced on him by his role will conflict with his personality." To her way of thinking, the individual will resolve the conflict in one of two ways—modify his personality to conform to the role considerations or leave the organization. In light of the hypothesized relationship between technical variables and organizational roles and the concomitant possibilities for conflict for the individual, Woodward concludes that perhaps top managers are brought to the upper levels of the organization through having those "personalities which best fit the technical background in which they have to operate."

Although explicit causal relationships were not defined, Woodward and her associates suggest that a number of other initial observations could be made from analyzing the results of this first survey. It was determined, for instance, that certain technical environments seem to impose greater strains than others might on members of all levels of the hierarchy. In addition, intermanagerial and employee-employer relationships appeared to "be better at the extremes of the scale than they were in the middle; pressure was greatest in the middle and it seemed more important to build mechanisms into the organizational structure which would resolve the conflicts likely to occur." At this stage of the research Woodward summarizes the findings and their implications for formulating the next stage of the study.

> Thus it seems that an analysis of situational demands could lead not only to the development of better techniques for appraising organizational structure and for conscious planning, but also to an increased understanding of the personal qualities and skills required in different industrial situations, and to improved methods of training directed towards giving those concerned a better understanding of the strains and stresses associated with the roles they are likely to occupy (p. 80).

The case studies

In order to investigate some of their initial observations, the group undertook a more detailed case study of 20 selected firms in which manufacturing methods were either changing or mixed. It was felt that if technology and organization were linked in the manner suggested by the earlier findings, more difficult organizational challenges and problems would arise in firms with these characteristics. Therefore, they wanted to examine firms which were characterized as undergoing a change in production systems (caused by technological developments) and which might require that the formal organization be modified to adjust to a new set of situational demands.

Firms utilizing mixed production systems were also chosen for additional study because of the possibilities they presented for studying potentially incompatible situational demands arising from the technology. If these organizations were found to have conflicting situational demands, study of the organizational structure might reveal the way in which these demands might be reconciled. Thus, this phase of the study was intended to evaluate in more detail the relationship between the technology of production and the associated organizational pattern. Consequently, the three main aspects of organization selected for examination in this phase of the study were: "the type of organization with particular reference to the breakdown between line and staff roles; the relationships between the three main functions of manufacturing—research and development, production, and marketing; and the organization of production, including the way in which results were predicted and controlled."

The researchers began by examining the relationship between situational demands arising from the technology and the organizational structure. In general, the "follow-up studies confirmed that in many firms the conscious process of organization-building proceeds independently of technical change and development, and that the link between technology and organization was not the product of conscious behavior or deliberate policy." In fact, many of those interviewed seemed to feel that there was no one best way for organizing a firm and that there were a number of alternatives which could potentially be as effective as the one they happened to be using. It appeared in some firms, that there were changes in organization which followed a change in technology and resulted from the apparent inability of the preceding organization to cope with that change.

Although the observations made in the second phase of the research seemed to support the conclusions of the initial study, a number of interesting points emerged in the more detailed phase of analysis. "The research workers realized as they studied firms more deeply that not only the type of organization but also the functions of the organization were linked with technology." Although the organization is often thought of as having a dual function in serving both technical and social ends, Woodward and her colleagues found rather substantial differences between the functions of organization required for one type of firm (or production process) and those of a firm utilizing a less advanced system of production. They discovered that, "In the process industry, the design or mechanism for coordinating work is intrinsic in the plant itself, and in some of the mass production firms they studied, the control system fulfilled a similar function." Consequently, "in both these systems, production emerged almost automatically once the production process had been set in motion." Summarizing the relationship between organization structure, functions, and technology among observed firms, Woodward states:

> This means that in the technically advanced firm organization serves primarily social ends, its function being to define roles and relationships within a social system. This means that the organization planner can concentrate on establishing the network of relationships which is best for people. Moreover, because coordination is independent of organization, the form of organization is not likely to have a critical effect on business success.
>
> In the less advanced systems of production, where organization serves both technical and social ends, there is likely to be a much closer link between business success and the form of organization, and the two functions can come into conflict. The network of relationships best for production is not necessarily best for people (p. 123).

Based on these observations, Woodward suggests that the initial step in designing an organizational structure compatible with the situational demands imposed by the technology, is to determine the purposes of the organization. Unfortunately, according to Woodward's view, classical management thought is inadequate in relating organizational structure to business success in this manner, particularly, when considered in light of the situational demands imposed by a particular technology.

After having made the distinction between task and element functions and their relationship to organizational structure, Woodward turned her analysis toward examining the relationship between the task functions and the personnel charged with carrying them out. This phase of the analysis focused on the relationship between task functions and the three major manufacturing tasks mentioned earlier: manufacturing, marketing, and development. In evaluating the task functions associated with each of these functions, Woodward and her colleagues discovered that in the technically advanced systems, the functions could be separated quite easily; however, in the unit and small-batch process firms, the separation between these three functions was much more difficult to achieve.

In addition, they determined that "the relative importance of the various functions was also related to the system of production," and that within each production organization, one task element seemed to be central and critical to both success and survival. Although they recognized that this difference in emphasis between firms could certainly be due to more than a dependency on a certain type of technology, they concluded that "in the long run, technology remained the dominant factor in the determination of the critical factor."

Through their analysis of the status system, they observed that the successful firms accorded adequate recognition to the importance of the critical function. They also discovered that the department in which the chief executive had previously worked was also the department with the highest status. Taking this link between the status system and technology as well as the background of the chief executive, they concluded that "there was a tendency for firms whose chief executive had been closely associated with the critical function earlier in his career to be the more successful ones."

The general outcome of this phase of the study can be summarized as follows:

> As we have seen, in unit production and large-batch and mass-production, organization has to serve both technical and social ends; the coordination of basic activities depends upon organization, the difference between these two types of production being that whereas in unit production there is no conflict between technical and social ends, in large-batch and mass production such conflict can and does arise.
>
> Process production is different again. This is the type of industry where organization does not have to provide a mechanism for the coordination of work; its main purpose is therefore social.
>
> The fact that organization does not provide the mechanism for the coordination of work may be the fundamental reason why relationships between development, production, and marketing were more harmonious in process firms than in large-batch and mass-production firms even though roles were in general less clearly defined (p. 127).

When the researchers turned their attention from the overall organizational structure to the more detailed elements of planning and controlling production, they found that the link between technology and organization was not always as apparent. When production organization was considered, it did not appear to be as closely related to technology as some of the other aspects of organization. In evaluating this situation further, Woodward and her colleagues observed that "there was greater variation in the way production operations were planned and controlled in the firms in the middle ranges of the scale. . . . As far as the organization of production was concerned, situational demands impose themselves more rigidly and obviously at the extremes than in the middle ranges of the scale.

It appeared that at either end of the continuum, the possible ranges in organizational choice were much more confined by the type of production technology than in the middle ranges; consequently, those in the middle ground had much more latitude in determining organizational issues related to production. In fact, it was determined that within this middle range, even an unsuitable organization had relatively little immediate impact on the success of the enterprise. Therefore, Woodward concludes that, in the case of firms in the middle ranges of the production spectrum, technology was an important variable; however, other variables were equally important.

It was in her analysis of the production organization that Woodward seemed to find classical management theory most noticeably inadequate for analyzing and understanding the behavior and the relationships associated with complicated production processes. Although the conventional line-staff classifications were evidently useful to the researchers in identifying and categorizing some of the problem areas in organization, they were unable to utilize these concepts in fully explaining the nature of their findings. This seemed to be particularly evident in those situations where they were attempting to evaluate the relationship between control systems and the human relations problems they observed in several situations.

The follow-up investigations

Throughout their extensive study of manufacturing organizations in the South Essex area, Woodward and her associates had demonstrated and evaluated the existence of a link between technology and organizational characteristics. They were now interested in deepening their understanding of the apparent interaction between technical and behavioral factors. To this end, additional and more intensive studies of three firms were begun. The researchers now wanted to refine the instrument used in classifying technology and detail the appropriate technical characteristics for the various production processes considered earlier. In addition, they wanted to further examine the relationship between technology and organization in those enterprises undergoing technical changes. One other objective of the study was to further examine the effects of formalization on control procedures.

The analysis of the control system was, to some degree, meant to serve as a basis for further studies in the area, and some comments on the background of this aspect of the project seem appropriate.

> Briefly, this project is based on the assumption that when the management of a firm makes a decision to manufacture a product or series of products a control system is automatically brought into existence. Objectives have to be determined in relation to the product and a sequence of activities planned in order to achieve these objectives. Plans then have to be executed and information generated to enable the results to be assessed. If activities are to be repeated, corrective action may have to be taken or the objectives modified in the light of the result obtained. For those concerned with the product at all levels of the hierarchy, the control system is the framework in which they

operate, determining the amount of discretion they have in the organization of their own activities. It is hoped that some way of describing control systems in terms of such parameters as degrees of formalization, complexity, and fragmentation will be found, and the behavior associated with them analyzed (p. 186).

The researchers discovered that substantially less organizational disturbance and modification had resulted in the one firm which experienced a change in moving from process production to automated, continuous-flow production than occurred in the two plants characterized as having substantially different production technologies. This would seem to support their initial hypothesis that: "Technical changes involving a change in the nature of the production system have the greatest effect on organization and behavior."

In continuous-process production plants, the commercial success of the enterprise was more closely linked to the assurances of a long-range market potential for its products; therefore, the "number of imponderables was relatively few and the consequences of taking a particular course of action could be predicted with a certain degree of certainty." Although Woodward does not elaborate on the topic of uncertainty in markets as it might affect intra-firm organizational issues, she seems to suggest that the problems faced by some of the other firms—having different production technologies—may be related to the uncertainties in marketing of products and the interrelationship of those uncertainties with production scheduling, control, and plant organization and administration.

The role of the chief executive also differed among the three types of companies. Again, because of the rigid framework of control provided by the production process itself in process industries, relationships were characterized as being less stressful then those in the other two firms. In addition, although the members of the organization were working under a relatively rigid framework of control—based on the process technology— there appeared to be fewer complaints in this organization regarding limitations on individual action and authority. Interestingly, chief executives in the process production industry were observed as spending less time on purely technical matters than their counterparts in other firms. Since technical decisions in crisis situations were delegated to those with technical expertise and long-range planning decisions were too important to be left to one man, the observers felt that the chief executive in this industry was more involved in the social organization of the firm than his counterparts in other types of production plants.

In evaluating the other two plants which were moving into the batch-production type of technology from opposite ends of the continuum, results concerning the effect of change on these two organizations indicated that the most "recalcitrant problems of organization and behavior are likely to be found in the batch-production area of technology." Since it was anticipated that the problems in adjusting to change in each of these organizations would probably take a greater period of time than in the process industry and might prove to be more costly, the researchers were interested in examining further the relationship between the degree of adjustment required and the duration of the period of tension accompanying these changes. Since the researchers sought to study a "before and after" situation, and already had considerable data on these firms, these studies allowed the researchers to control the experiment somewhat by holding the factors other than technology constant.

In analyzing the results of this phase of the study, the researchers concluded that their initial predictions of the effect of technological change on organization and behavior were substantiated. In brief, they determined that the batch-production technology brought with it some of the most difficult problems in both behavior and organization. "Moreover, the differences in the ease with which firms adapted to technical change could be explained in terms of the senior managers' ability to anticipate these problems, and the initiative shown in simultaneous planning of organizational and technical change." According to Woodward, the results of this phase of the study:

> Provided a further demonstration of the main thesis put forward. . . , i.e., that meaningful explanations of behavior can be derived from an analysis of the work situation. It seemed that in identifying technology as one of the primary variables on which behavior depended, a step forward had been made in the determination of the conditions under which behavior becomes standardized and predictable (p. 208).

In evaluating the effects of technical change on organization and behavior, the researchers also examined the relationship between informal and formal organization within the firms being studied and found that the organizational objectives were frequently achieved by the informal organization. Furthermore, they found that "a disfunctional organization could be compensated by contributive informal relationships," and that this observation was particularly notable when viewed in relation to technical change.

When technical change was introduced, the researchers found that organizations varied in the way in which the formal and informal organizations responded to the new requirements. In some firms, where technical change and organizational change were simultaneously planned and initiated, adjustment of the informal to the formal organization seemed much more rapid. Conversely, where organizational change and technical change were not simultaneously introduced and/or planned for, the informal organization was the primary means by which the organizational goal was effected. It was only later that the adjustment was made in the formal organization. The possible advantages in control gained through proper attention to planning both organizational and technical change seem evident and appear to be supported by Woodward's analysis.

Conclusions

Certainly, the conclusions reached in the study tend to support the view that the "rules of classical management theory do not always work in practice"; however, classical theory was not dismissed as useless in the analysis of organizations.

Woodward concluded that the existing classical theory was deficient in its ability to incorporate the formal and informal aspects of organizational behavior. She also found the human relations school to be inadequate in explaining the complexities of organization and behavior. Consequently, "far from casting away management principles altogether, one of the more significant factors in the research findings was the confirmation that these principles were positively linked to business success in one particular area of technology." But there is still the absence of clearcut guides for application in differing settings which would enhance both stability in application and improved predictability.

James D. Thompson's
"Organizations in Action"

DONNA G. GOEHLE

James D. Thompson, in prefacing his *Organizations in Action* (34), states that "a central purpose of the book is to identify a framework which might link at important points several of the now independent approaches to understanding organizations." In developing primarily a theoretical inventory of concepts and propositions about the ways in which those concepts might be related in explaining complex organizations, Thompson does not attempt to test his formulations empirically; rather, he suggests that the framework he advances may be useful for others in generating those hypotheses. In contrast to Woodward's work, Thompson has included a wide range of organizational types which he generally characterizes as being "instrumental organizations which induce or coerce participation" and has excluded only those organizations of a "voluntary" nature such as some religious groups and ideological associations. From the outset, Thompson makes it clear that he is interested in focusing on the behavior of organizations and only tangentially in considering individual behavior within organizations.

Thompson has attempted to meld many of the various approaches to the study of organizations arising out of the various fields and disciplines which deal with observing and understanding complex organizations. According to Thompson, these interdisciplinary approaches have yielded useful concepts and propositions regarding organizations, though their contributions to the general field of organizational study have been limited by fragmentation. Therefore, rather than focusing entirely on one approach discarding critical elements of several different ones, Thompson suggests ways in which the approaches and concepts can be reconciled and used in building a more comprehensive theoretical framework which more accurately assists in explaining the complex phenomena involved in organizational analysis.

Strategies for studying organizations

Thompson begins his book by reviewing the complexities of organizations and the various conceptual approaches which have been developed in attempting to explain and understand the phenomena associated with complex organizations. He discusses the inherent conflict between the "closed-system" and "open-system" models and their apparent limitations in application. Finding both of these models lacking in comprehensiveness—the closed system in that it does not accommodate environmental influences and the open system in that it perhaps overemphasizes adaptability to the neglect of more controllable elements—Thompson indicates that the Simon-March-Cyert stream of study provides some means of overcoming the conflict between the two approaches. However, he also feels that this latter approach is lacking in that it tends to omit some of the useful information garnered from studies utilizing the older approaches.

Consequently, Thompson also attempts a synthesis of the closed and open systems approach in his treatment of organizational behavior. Thompson says, "For purposes of this volume then, we will conceive of complex organizations as open systems, hence indeterminate and faced with uncertainty, but at the same time subject to criteria of rationality, and hence needing determinateness and certainty." The remainder of the first section of his book is devoted to explaining the nature of the conflict between these two approaches and the necessity of viewing organizations in relation to concepts advanced in both the open and closed systems approaches. He recognizes that much of the literature illustrates the adaptiveness of organizations to their environment, and also recognizes the weakness of such approaches in application to organizational design and administrative practice. Therefore, he seeks some means of building upon these concepts while holding rationality as a criteria upon which the theory must also be judged.

He does not suggest that the two approaches are equally incompatible at all ranges of organizational phenomena, but that the problems associated with each tend to fall into one of Parson's three categories of responsibility and control—"technical, managerial, and institutional." For each of these levels, Thompson indicates that a different approach may be most suitable. For instance, "if the closed-system aspects of organizations are seen most clearly at the technical level, and the open-system qualities appear most vividly at the institutional level, it would suggest that a significant function of the managerial level is to mediate between the two extremes and the emphases they exhibit." Since organizations are usually forced to interact with their environment in both resource-acquisition and output disposal, Thompson argues that the organization will attempt to isolate its "technical core" as much as possible from the uncertainties generated by this interaction with the environment.

Because uncertainties may arise from either the technology or the environment, and since there are substantial numbers of variations observable in both categories, Thompson argues that organizations will also differ in their methods of coping with these different combinations. Since the three levels (technical, managerial, and institutional) are interdependent, organizational differences in coping with uncertainty of various types will also create differences in these levels across organizations as efforts are made to reduce uncertainty.

Rationality in organizations

In his chapter on rationality in organizations, Thompson attempts to develop a framework from which the relationship between "technical rationality" and "organizational rationality" can be understood, compared, and related to the actions of complex organizations.

According to him, "instrumental action is rooted on one hand in desired outcomes and on the other hand in beliefs about cause-effect relationships. Given a desire, the state of man's knowledge at any point in time dictates the kinds of variables required and the manner of their manipulation to bring that desire to fruitation." In Thompson's view, "technical rationality" represents "the extent to which these activities thus dictated by man's beliefs are judged to produce the desired outcomes." The measures of technical rationality can be evaluated in terms of whether or not the desired outcome is achieved (instrumental) and whether the results were achieved with the least expenditure of resources (economic). Both of these criteria are essential to a discussion of the ways in which technology may be employed by complex organizations, and consequently, its potential influence on the organization itself.

Since there are numerous technologies available in society which may be employed by organizations, three general categories of technology are proposed which are sufficiently distinct for purposes of illustrating Thompson's point. They are: *"long-linked* (involving serial independence); *mediating* (requiring operating in standardized ways and extensively with multiple clients or customers widely distributed in time and space); and *intensive* (a custom technology which depends on the availability of potentially necessary resources and their suitable application in an individual case or project.)"

According to Thompson, since technical rationality is an abstraction concerning beliefs about cause and effect relationships, "it is only instrumentally perfect when it becomes a closed system of logic." Since organizations are forced to implement these technologies in action, the logic of the closed system does not accurately reflect the requirements nor the alternatives characterizing particular situations. Therefore, although every organization can be described as having a "core technology," the "technical core is always an incomplete representation of what the organization must do to accomplish desired results." And according to Thompson:

> Technical rationality is a necessary component but never alone sufficient to provide *organizational rationality* which involves acquiring

the inputs which are taken for granted by the technology, and dispensing outputs which again are outside the scope of the core technology. At a minimum, organizational rationality involves three major component activities: (1) input activities, (2) technological activities, and (3) output activities. Since they are interdependent, organizational rationality requires that they be appropriately geared to one another. The inputs acquired must be within the scope of the technology, and it must be within the capacity of the organization to dispose of the technological production (p. 19).

Given this interdependence, it is obvious that the input and output activities require an open-system type of logic and do impinge on the closed-system logic of the technology. Because of this interdependence, it is impossible to completely "seal-off" the technological core in the sense of a closed-system. Therefore, organizations will seek to minimize the influences of the environment through such techniques as buffering, leveling, forecasting, and rationing. The elements within the environment which Thompson feels are an influence on organizational action can be classified as "constraints" and "contingencies." Constraints are those fixed conditions which the organization cannot control. Contingencies are those factors which may or may not vary but are not subject to the arbitrary control of the organization. Organizational rationality is, therefore, some combination of constraints, contingencies, and the controllable variables cited previously.

Because it is assumed that organizations will seek some types of control over environmental interdependence and will engage in various types of action to gain that control where possible, Thompson suggests that the direction of those actions as well as the nature of them must also be examined. In order to accomplish that task, he introduces the concept of organizational "domain."

Domains of organized action

Organizations must establish some type of domain in terms of the "range of products, the populations served, and the services offered." He then goes on to consider the relationship between domain, dependence, and environment. In Thompson's words "The results of organizational action rest not on a single technology, but upon a technological matrix. A complicated technology incorporates the products or results of still other technologies. Although a particular organization may operate several core technologies, its domain always falls short of the total matrix."

With such a concept, Thompson illustrates the interlocking relationships among modern organizations in general, and commercial enterprises in particular. Given these overlaps within the system, "the organization's domain identifies the points at which the organization is dependent on inputs from the environment." The nature of the dependencies, for a particular organization, will be primarily determined by the composition of the environment and the location of various organization-serving capacities within it. Thus, the organizational interfaces with the environment—such as sources of raw materials and markets for products—can be viewed as being dispersed, concentrated, or somewhere between the two extremes. According to Thompson, each organization will have a unique set of input and output relationships depending on the environment which it encounters and operates within.

Since environment can be taken to mean almost everything beyond the internal organization, he suggests that William R. Dill's concept of "task environment," which defines task environment as "the parts of the environment which are relevant or potentially relevant to goal setting and goal attainment," is more useful conceptually. Among the elements of task environment are the following: customers, suppliers, competitors, and regulatory groups. In the same way that no two organizational domains are exactly alike, neither are two task environments. In Thompson's view, "which individuals, which other organizations, and which aggregates constitute the task environment for a particular organization is determined by the requirements of the technology, the boundaries of the domain, and the composition of the larger environment."

In examining the relationship between task environment and domain, he argues that domain-consensus is reached through mutual expectations regarding the roles of various organizations. This consensus "defines a set of expectations both for members of the organization and for others with whom they interact about what the organization will and will not do." This appears to be one of the weaker arguments in the discussion thus far, since Thompson does not deal with the fact that different elements of the task environment may have widely divergent views regarding the domain of other elements. For example, he mentions regulatory agencies as being one of the elements of a firm's task environment along with customers, suppliers, competitors, etc., but he argues that domain consensus arises from mutual expectations about what others will and/or will not do. It would seem that each of these elements may have very different expectations about what the firm will or will not do. In fact, perhaps, it is this lack of consensus on specifics which requires the existence of regulatory agencies to continually redefine the boundaries of the firm's domain. On the other hand, the firm may have very different expectations of the appropriate domain for regulatory agencies and for its intermediate customers, to mention only two areas of potential disagreement.

Still, each organization must exchange with several elements of its task environment, each of which is also involved in a network of interdependencies characterizing its own domain and task environment. In this process of multiorganizational interaction, one or more elements in the task environment of one organization may choose to discontinue its support of that organization. Thus, according to Thompson, task environments also impose contingencies for organizations. In addition, they may also impose constraints, such as those encountered by a local high school which can only draw on the surrounding community for certain inputs. Since both constraints and contingencies can interfere with the attainment of rationality, Thompson argues that "organizations that are subject to the norms of rationality will attempt to manage dependency."

In order to manage that dependency, organizations must have some kind of power. To Thompson, power is the obverse of dependence. In his view, "an organization has power relative to an element of its task environment, to the extent that the organization has capacity to satisfy the needs of that element and to the extent that the organization monopolizes that capacity." An organization's "net power" results from the interaction of the organization with the various elements comprising the pluralistic task environment. In this view, organizations with relatively little control over inputs will seek to gain power on the output side of the equation.

Some organizations will also be characterized as being powerful or weak in their ability to control *both* inputs and outputs; however, those organizations gaining control over both inputs and outputs may find that countervailing power may arise within the task environment to reduce the discretion with which that power might be applied (i.e., regulatory agencies). Thompson also argues that power should not be treated as a zero-sum game in that increased interdependence among equally powerful elements may result in increased power for both parties.

Organizations want to manage the dependency of their task environment, and there are several strategies they can follow to avoid becoming subservient to any of the elements in that environment. The organization may attempt to maintain alternatives (as in the case of suppliers), acquire "prestige" (one of the "cheapest" means of gaining power since it does not increase dependency), enlarge the task environment, and engage in cooperative strategies for managing interdependencies (such as contracting, coopting, and coalescing). In attempting to manage interorganizational relations and maintain a viable domain, organizations are seeking an "optimal point between the realities of interdependence and the norms of rationality." Since the maneuvering necessary to reach that optimum point can be both costly and disruptive, organizations "subject to norms of rationality [would] seek to design themselves so as to minimize the necessity of maneuvering and compromise."

Organizational design

In addition to dealing with contingencies through developing strategies for interaction with the elements of the task environment, Thompson argues that organizations may also be able to remove or reduce those contingencies through organizational design. Since the domain of an organization is influenced by technology, the population being served and the services being rendered, a substantial change in organizational design would involve a modification of the "mix" of these elements. Some of the ways in which this modification might be achieved include vertical integration (especially with long-linked technologies), increases in the size of the populations being served (as in mediating technologies), and incorporating the object or the client into the organization (as in the case of intensive technologies). Not all of these alternatives are viable for an organization at any one time since organizations may be constrained by capital requirements, the ability of the market to absorb additional production output, and/or legal restrictions, to mention only a few.

Nevertheless, if we assume there are pressures being exerted on the organization which encourage it to grow, Thompson argues that the direction of growth will "not be random but will be guided by the nature of the technology and the task environment. Consequently, if organizations vary in design, they must also vary in structure".

Technology and structure

In introducing the topic of organizational structure, Thompson states:

The major components of a complex organization are determined by the design of that organization. Invariably these major components are further segmented, or departmentalized, and connections are established within and between departments. It is this internal differentiation and patterning of relationships that we will refer to as structure (p. 51).

He is particularly interested in considering those components of the organization which appear to be most protected from environmental influences—the technical core. (The combined effects of both environment and technology are dealt with later in his work.) Since "structure is a fundamental vehicle by which organizations achieve bounded rationality," some coordination of effort, along with protection of the technical core is achieved.

By delimiting responsibilities, control over resources, and other matters, organizations provide their participating members with boundaries within which efficiency may be a reasonable expectation. But if structure affords numerous spheres of bounded rationality, it must also facilitate the *coordinated* action of those *independent* elements (p. 54).

Thus, according to Thompson, before organizational structure can be understood, the meaning of, and different types of interdependence and coordination must be considered. Three types of internal interdependence described by Thompson include "pooled interdependence," "sequential interdependence," and "reciprocal interdependence." These three types, in the order introduced, contain increasing degrees of contingency and are, therefore, more difficult and costly to coordinate. The three methods of coordination, each most appropriate for dealing with the different types of interdependence, are "standardization," "coordination by plan," and "coordination by mutual adjustment." Since coordination is necessary, but may also be costly, Thompson argues that organizations will seek to minimize coordination costs. "It is the task of structure to facilitate the appropriate coordinating processes."

Operating under norms of rationality and in attempting to minimize coordination costs, organizations will localize and make "conditionally autonomous, first reciprocally then sequentially interdependent ones, and finally grouping positions homogeneously to facilitate standardization." Hierarchy is introduced because of the fact that first groupings do not totally take care of interdependence. Therefore, the organization must find some means of linking the groups involved into higher-order groups, or, in effect, establishing a hierarchy. Any interdependence not included by these arrangements will then require the establishment of committees or task forces to overcome the problems of coordination.

Organization and structure

Since complex organizations must interface with their environment, yet cannot fully control the influences arising from those interdependencies, the structure of the boundary-spanning units within an organization must allow for the necessary adjustments to continue to be made. In this section of his book, Thompson deals with the way in which environment also influences organizational structure (especially in the structure of the boundary-spanning units) as well as the way in which both technology and environment together influence the overall structure of the organization.

Although Thompson recognizes that the elements of the task environment vary for different organizations and, therefore, introduce certain constraints which are unique to that organization, he argues that generally the nature of those constraints can be classified within two major categories: "geographic space" (such as the costs involved in transportation) and in the "social composition" of their task environment. The social composition of the task environment can be viewed as being homogeneous or heterogeneous and stable or shifting. According to Thompson, "all organizations face task environments which are simultaneously located somewhere on the homogeneous-heterogeneous continuum and the stable-shifting continuum."

In summarizing the impact of the task environment on the structure of boundary-spanning units, Thompson states:

> The more heterogeneous the task environment, the greater the constraints presented to the organization. The more dynamic the task environment, the greater the contingencies presented to the organization. Under either condition, the organization seeking to be rational must put boundaries around the amount and scope of adaption necessary, and it does this by establishing structural units specialized to face a limited range of contingencies within a limited set of contraints. The more constraints and contingencies the organization faces, the more its boundary-spanning component will be segmented (p. 73).

Having considered the influences on the structure of the units comprising the "technical core" and the "boundary-spanning" units, the concern then becomes the means by which these elements are combined to result in the overall organizational structure. Those organizations characterized as having "technical cores and boundary-spanning activities which can be isolated from each other will be centralized with an overarching layer of functional divisions." Where those activities are reciprocally interdependent rather than isolated, an organization will tend toward arranging these units in self-sufficient clusters, each having its own domain; "this is the major form of decentralization."

Thus, in Thompson's view, the organization faces internal

requirements for coordinating the technical core and externally-generated requirements for adjustment of the boundary-spanning units to the contingencies and constraints of the environment. Therefore, the major purpose of structure is to allow for the satisfaction of both internal and external organizational requirements. Because he assumes bounded rationality is necessary, Thompson argues that organizations facing heterogeneous task environments will not only attempt to identify homogeneous elements in that environment but also will establish structural units capable of dealing with each type. In this way, Thompson attempts to tie together the structural implications of the apparently incompatible close-system and open-system requirements.

The variable human

Thompson then turns to a discussion of the characteristics of individuals and how they relate to organizations. He considers such things as the extent to which organizations can increase predictability of the behavior of their members and/or others in the task environment. He also discusses, in considerable detail, the exercise of discretion on the part of organizational members. A central argument is that "the ability or opportunity to exercise discretion is not uniformly distributed throughout the organization—that technology, task environment, design, and structure result in patterns of discretion." Thompson is interested in identifying the participants who exercise discretion, the relationships among those individuals, what "discretion" implies, and how it might be expressed or exercised.

Since Thompson has indicated from the outset that his focus is primarily on the behavior of organizations in a general sense, rather than on the behavior of specific individuals within those organizations, this second section of his text builds extensively on the preceding organizational concepts and relationships which have already been discussed.

In viewing organization members, Thompson sees them as having certain aspirations and beliefs about cause and effect relationships and postulates that they (the individuals) bring these with them to an organizational setting which provides compatible opportunities and constraints. Culture, in his view, tends to be an "homogenizing" force which limits the range of diversity of these beliefs and aspirations and allows for the "channeling" of these individuals into relevant sectors of the labor market. He argues that the composition of the inducements/contribution contract is influenced by these factors and that the I/C contract itself further limits the range of behavior an individual will exhibit in an organizational setting. All of these factors, when taken together, tend to reduce the potential for heterogeneity of expression among organizational members.

Given these observations, the individual's range of discretion can be viewed in the context of "spheres of action." These action spheres also, "differ according to the technologies in which these jobs are imbedded." By locating jobs within technological contexts, individuals are therefore presented with patterned spheres of action." Since a job is "both a unit in the organization and a unit in the career of the individual, the joining of the two is a result of bargained agreement or inducements/contribution contract." Given the duality of the expectations, "it is then only reasonable to expect the resulting behavior to be patterned."

Proceeding from these initial assumptions regarding the nature of the individual behavior in an organizational setting, Thompson further illustrates the ways in which these patterns of behavior are influenced by technological factors, environmental constraints and contingencies, and the individual's position within the subunits of the organizational structure. He builds on the concepts of interdependence and power to describe the range of discretion and/or authority for an individual. In this manner, Thompson integrates a logical framework of individual behavior within the overall framework already established for the organization.

The administrative process is considered in terms of two types of administrative action necessary for the organization to survive. They are "adaptive" and "directive." Adaptive actions are necessitated primarily by environmental influences, and directive actions arise out of the basic internal requirements of the organization. Recognizing that both types of action are necessary, they must be coordinated in such a way as to allow the organization to manipulate "strategic variables" in order to survive. This manipulation of strategic variables should, therefore, result in a "viable co-alignment" with other elements in the environment. Given the fluidity of the task environment, it is apparent that the types of co-alignment are continually changing; therefore, a major task of administration, in Thompson's view, is to reduce the uncertainty involved in the process through achieving co-alignment "not merely of people (in coalitions) but of institutionalized action—of technology and task environment into a viable domain, and of organizational structure appropriate to it." As a result, "the administrative process must reduce uncertainty but at the same time search for flexibility."

Conclusions

Thompson concludes that the fundamental problem faced by complex organizations is coping with uncertainty. Coping with uncertainty is therefore the essence of the administrative process. The sources of uncertainty for an organization arise from three areas, two are external to the organization and one is internal. "External uncertainties stem from (1) *generalized uncertainty* or lack of cause/effect understanding of the culture at large, and (2) contingency, in which the outcomes of organizational action are in part determined by the actions of elements of the environment." The third source of uncertainty is internal; the *interdependence of components*. The way in which these uncertainties are resolved is:

> Solution of the first type [generalized uncertainty], provides a pattern against which organizational action can be ordered. Solution of the second type [contingency] affords organizational freedom to so order

the action against the pattern. Solution of the third [interdependence of components] results in the actual ordering of action to fit the pattern. (p. 160).

This is the way Thompson summarizes the general nature of his view of organizations as having certain aspects of closed systems and of open systems within a context of internal and external uncertainty. Given the assumed necessity of rationality, both must be taken individually and together in explaining the behavior of complex organizations in a contemporary setting.

Organization Analysis: A Sociological Point of View

CHARLES PERROW

The mixed model

Let us assume, for a moment, that we are talking about organizations where all three of the following functions are important: research, production, and marketing. Though industrial terminology is being used here, it should be recognized that all organizations have, to at least some limited extent, all these functions. A correctional institution, an employment agency, the social security administration, or various military units all not only produce products but must also market them in some form or other. The manner in which they produce and market these products is based upon an appropriate technology. To find, change, develop, and improve the technology constitutes a research function, as does the determination of what the new products will be. Of course, for some organizations, marketing is a minor problem, while for others it is a major one, and the same is true of research and even of production. Assuming all three are important, however, how should they be organized?

The organizational form will depend upon the state of the art in each function and the changes required by the environment. Preferably production and marketing would be routinized: even fairly routine research functions would be preferred. . . . If all three are routine (or nonroutine), the organization has little difficulty in determining the best

From *Organizational Analysis: A Sociological View* by Charles Perrow, © 1970 by Wadsworth Publishing Company, Inc., Belmont, California 94002. Reprinted by permission of the author and the publisher, Brooks/Cole Publishing Company.

method of organizing the whole. All can be structured alike and integration problems are minimized.

However, it is far more common to find varying degrees of routinization among the three functions. Typically, production is fairly routine and exists in a stable environment; research is nonroutine; and marketing is in-between. This situation presents problems of coordination beyond those normally encountered when there are different units, since the three units will think differently and will be accustomed to different ways of getting things done. Production, for example, may think only in terms of the very short run. This is the basis upon which this function is judged; the unit is not responsible for, nor in a position to anticipate, new products or techniques. Marketing, however, must take a somewhat longer perspective. (If the marketing function is not developed, and only a sales division exists, its perspective may be as short-range as production.) Development, and especially research, however, should have a relatively long perspective compared to production and marketing. Time perspectives establish priorities, and thus the units may clash. They will disagree about such matters as the allocation of resources or the urgency of solving a particular problem. Not only perspectives are involved, but also actual structures. With its short-range perspective and precise goals which can be measured, production is likely to have highly specialized subunits, clear lines of authority, precise rules and procedures. Research, at the other extreme, may depend more upon lateral and diagonal communication among its members, resulting in a good deal of informal contact; there may be few intermediate measures of productivity and few binding rules or procedures. It may be difficult for members of these two departments to work together, or even to communicate information easily, because of their different "styles."

Technology models

So far we have been content with a simple polar contrast between bureaucratized organizations or units and nonbureaucratized units. The key to the distinction has been the kind of work performed in the organization or unit of the organization: its degree of routine or lack of routine. But if we analyze the term "routine" more closely, it appears that we mean that two conditions are present—there are well-established techniques which are sure to work, and these are applied to essentially similar raw materials. That is, there is little uncertainty about methods and little variety or change in the tasks that must be performed.

Similarly, nonroutineness means that there are a few well-established techniques; there is little certainty about methods, or whether or not they will work. But it also means that there may be a variety of different tasks to perform, in the sense that raw materials are not standardized, or orders from customers ask for many different or custom-made products.

The operations of some firms may have little variety, yet quite a bit of uncertainty; others may have little uncertainty, but a great deal of variety. These two types are neither highly routine nor highly nonroutine. They are in the middle somehow, but they are not in the same middle; they themselves differ from one another. So it is possible to be nonroutine in one sense and not another, or routine in one sense but not in another. . . .

Variability and search. . . . Organizations are designed to get some kind of work done. To do this work they need techniques or technologies. These techniques are applied to some kind of "raw material" which the organization transforms into a marketable product. It doesn't matter what the product is; it may be reformed delinquents, TV programs, advertising symbols, governmental decisions, or steel. But some technology is required, not only in the actual production process, but also for procuring the input of materials, capital, and labor and disposing of the output to some other organization or consumer, and for coordinating the three "functions" or "phases" of input-transformation-output.

How does one think about, or conceptualize technology so that it may be analyzed in this way, as a means of transforming raw materials (human, symbolic, or material) into desirable goods and services? In this view of technology, machines and equipment are merely tools; they are not the technology itself. Indeed, the personnel man uses a technology that has little to do with tools. Nor can we use the actual techniques such as are found in production manuals, for these are too specific to the particular organization. Instead, let us consider the individual who is assigned to do a specific task.

He receives stimuli (orders, signals) to which he must respond. Even the decision to ignore the stimulus or not even to "see it" is a response. He "searches" his mind to decide what kind of response to make. So far we have two concepts with which to work: the stimulus and the response. The response is conceived of as "search behavior": If the stimulus is familiar and the individual has learned in the past what to do in the face of it, little search behavior is required. He may respond automatically or after a moment's thought. . . .

If the stimulus is unfamiliar, however, and the individual decides not to ignore it or to panic, considerable search behavior must be instituted, and the search is of a different kind. The problem presented by the stimulus is not immediately analyzable; search must take place without manuals, computers, or clerks who have the requisite information and programs. . . .

If we substitute a more general term for stimuli—raw material—we can see that the nature of the search procedure depends a good deal upon what is known about the material that one is to transform through techniques. If a good deal is known that is relevant to the transformation process, search can be quite routine and analyzable. . . .

The other dimension of technology which will be used here is the variability of the stimuli presented to an individual—the variety of problems which may lead to search behavior. Sometimes the variety is great and every task seems to be a new one demanding the institution of search behavior of some magnitude (whether analyzable or unanalyzable). Sometimes stimuli are not very varied and the individual is confronted chiefly with familiar situations and a few novel ones. Note that, in industrial firms, this is not necessarily a distinction between a great or small variety of products. Automobile firms produce an amazing variety of models and a

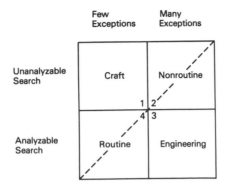

Figure 1. Technology Variables

staggering variety of parts, but these are not novel situations requiring search behavior (except in the design and engineering of model changes).

Note that if one were discussing only routine and nonroutine companies or bureaucratic and nonbureaucratic structures, only cells 4 and 2 would be distinction between technologically advanced and technologically backward industries. Some semiconductors, such as auto diodes, are a product of advanced technology but they can be made in a quite routine fashion. Certain kinds of ferro castings for the auto industry—a technologically "backward" process—cannot be made on a routine basis. To routinize production would require the solution of problems that have yet to be analyzed.

We now have two dimensions, the degree of variability of stimuli and the degree to which search procedures are analyzable. Let us refer to the first as simply the number of *exceptions* encountered by the individual. If we dichotomize and then cross-classify these there are four possibilities which, in Figure 1, we have labeled craft, nonroutine, routine, and engineering.

A factory manufacturing a standard product like heating elements for electric stoves (cell 4), and an engineering firm building made-to-order machines such as drill presses or electric motors (cell 3), may both be routine to the extent to which search behavior is analyzable. Still, they differ in the variety of occasions when search must be instituted—rarely in the factory, and quite frequently in the engineering firm. The engineering firm must continually modify designs and introduce modifications to meet the customers' needs. In a firm making fine glassware (cell 1), search may be as unanalyzable as in the factory which makes nuclear-propulsion systems (cell 2). Yet the variety of the stimuli in the glassware factory is small, while the varying requirements of the customers of the other firm present a great variety of problems or stimuli. The work of the nuclear fuel system firm would be highly nonroutine, combining unanalyzable problems with great variability of problems; the operations of a heating-element factory or a mill making reinforcing bars for concrete structure would be highly routine—a small variety of problems, while those which do occur would be subject to analyzable search procedures. The glass firm is low on variability but high on unanalyzable search procedures (therefore, referred to as a craftsman model). The engineering firm is high on variability but has analyzable search procedures—an engineering model.

Note that if one were discussing only routine and nonroutine companies or bureaucratic and nonbureaucratic structures, only cells 4 and 2 would be relevant. These are represented by a two-dimensional continuum characterized by a broken line; this is the sort of operation to which we have previously limited our discussion. However, organizations can fall into the categories represented by cells 1 and 3 though they probably would cluster rather close to the center of the figure.

The same kind of analysis can be used for people-changing organizations. . . .

Technology and structure. What, then does technology have to do with the *structure* of the organization? The answer has already been strongly hinted at in the discussion of nonbureaucratic and bureaucratic structures. But now it is possible to be a little more specific. We must assume here that, in the interest of efficiency, organizations wittingly or unwittingly attempt to maximize the congruence between their technology and their structure. Many which fail to make such a match should be more or less bureaucratically organized than they are. But let us assume that they have all studied the sociology of complex organizations and have adapted their structures to fit their technology. What would the four types of firms look like?

There are many, many ways to conceptualize structure. For our purposes here let me choose the following variables: the discretion of subgroups; their power; the basis of coordination within a group; and the interdependence of groups. For the moment, let us also deal only with production, although these concepts are equally applicable to marketing and perhaps even to the research aspects of organizations. If we single out middle and lower management we can make some predictions about the organization of each group and the relationship between them. Middle management here will, in general, mean the people who are concerned with the administration of production; we will call this the technical level. Lower management is concerned with the supervision of production.

Figure 2 suggests some of the structural characteristics of the four types of firms. In the nonroutine type of firm—characterized by unanalyzable search procedures and the need to deal with many exceptions—both discretion and power are high in both groups; in both, coordination is through feedback (mutual adjustment) rather than through advance planning (programmed), and finally, the interdependence of the groups is high. What this means is that the supervisors of production work closely with the technical people in the administration of production since the latter cannot call the shots for the former on the basis of routine information sent upstairs. Indeed, job descriptions may be such that it is difficult to distinguish the supervisory level from the technical level. Both groups are free to define situations as best they can. Therefore, both have

	Discretion	Power	Coordination within Groups	Interdependence of Groups	Discretion	Power	Coordination within Groups	Interdependence of Groups
Technical	Low	Low	Plan		High	High	Feed	
				Low				High
Supervision	High	High	Feed		High	High	Feed	
				Decentralized				Flexible, polycentralized
				1	2			
				4	3			
Technical	Low	High	Plan		High	High	Feed	
				Low				Low
Supervision	Low	Low	Plan		Low	Low	Plan	
				Formal, centralized				Flexible, centralized

Figure 2. Task Structure—Task-related Interaction

considerable power with respect to such matters as resources and organizational strategies.

This model resembles what others have called the organic as opposed to the mechanistic structure, or the professional or collegial as opposed to the bureaucratic structure. This type of structure is probably efficient only for highly nonroutine organizations. There are few of these, even though they are quite visible and attractive to social scientists who see in them reflections of their academic institutions and values.

Most firms fit into the quite routine cell. It is in their interest to fall in this category because it means greater control over processes and much more certainty of outlook (we are ignoring market situations). In routine firms, the discretion allowed to both supervisors of production and administrators of production is minimal—there is little ambiguity in these situations. The power of the technical middle-management level, however, is high, for it controls the supervisory level on the basis of routine reports. In both cases coordination within the levels comes through planning (giving further power to the technical level) because events can be foreseen. Interdependence between the two groups is likely to be low. This arrangement approaches the bureaucratic model. Where it is appropriate, it is undoubtedly the most efficient.

In the engineering model—characterized by analyzable problems with many exceptions—the technical-level functions more like the nonroutine

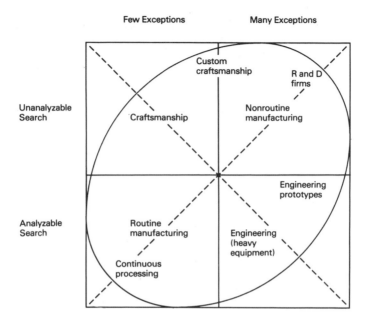

Figure 3.

firm. There is great discretion in choosing among programs, and considerable power, and coordination is achieved through the feedback of information for problem solving. But on the shop floor, discretion and power are—should be—minimal. Planning is the basis of coordination here, and there is little interdependence between the two levels—designs are sent down and executed. In the craftsman model—characterized by unanalyzable problems and a few exceptions—it is the supervisory level which has discretion and high power and coordinates through feedback. The technical level is weak, responds to the supervisors of production, and needs little discretion and little power. Coordination is on the basis of planning in the technical level. Interdependence of the two levels can be low.

To become even bolder in our speculation, Figure 3 may be revised to include two more unusual types of industrial organizations—the research and development firm or unit, which would be very nonroutine, and the continuous processing industry, such as oil or chemicals, or, to some extent, beer and other beverages, which would be very routine. Other examples of craft and engineering firms can also be added. (See figure 3).

The elliptical character of the model suggests that it is somewhat unusual to find organizations at the extreme of the axis represented by the dotted line. Still, examples do exist on that continuum. The distinction is not simply between routine and nonroutine or between bureaucratic and nonbureaucratic, as represented by the broken line.

This analysis is, admittedly, entirely speculative.[1] However, research is proceeding along these lines, and there may be some support for the specific models and predictions. We have gone into this particular theory in such detail in order to suggest at least one way of conceptualizing differences among organizations and to show that these differences indicate different kinds of strategies, none of which are either good or bad in themselves. As noted, most social scientists consider the nonbureaucratic, or nonroutine organization to be good and the bureaucratic or routine organization to be bad (it impedes progress, is old-fashioned, is hard on its employees, etc.).[2] But this judgment is debatable. One of the purposes of the R and D firm, or the nonroutine organization, is to generate ways of routinizing production and building better bureaucratic controls into organizations. Furthermore, for routine work, the bureaucratic structure may be both the most efficient and the most humane. Not all people prefer the hectic, open-ended, and uncertain character of nonroutine tasks, not even top management.

In addition, this little exercise in speculation suggests a way of looking at problems in organizational structure. For example, going back to figure 1, to simplify matters, if an organization in cell 1 (craft) hires an engineer at the middle management level who is used to working an organization in cell 3 (engineering), and if he tries through the use of discretion and personal power to coordinate the work in his unit by means of on-the-spot feedback, he is likely to be in for trouble. In this type of firm, many production problems have no analyzable solution. An engineer cannot dictate the solution of such problems nor can he exercise a high degree of discretion in helping or controlling staff members at the supervisory level. Furthermore, because problems vary very little and exceptional occasions seldom occur, he will find that he must do a great deal more advance planning within the technical group in order to support the supervisory level. He cannot expect supervisors to coordinate their own activities primarily through advance planning because of the unanalyzable nature of the problems which do occur.

Or, suppose that a successful production supervisor from a firm in cell 4 (routine) is moved to a position in a different division of the company where the work is more characteristic of cell 2 activities (nonroutine). Such a supervisor might find it quite difficult to become accustomed to exercising a high degree of discretion and power within this supervisory level. He might also be unable to adjust to coordination achieved through on-the-spot discussion when he has been used to coordination by means of fairly routine advance planning.

However, these examples relate to the problems of individuals. A more striking instance might be a case involving the recommendations of a management consultant firm which is accustomed to dealing with organizations within cell 4 (routine). Should the consultants try to apply their customary solutions to an organization in one of the other cells, they well might fail. (The Hoover Commission, charged with reorganizing much of the federal government, consistently made this error.) Similarly, a management-training program designed to increase the independence and autonomy of managers and the interdependence of groups could be quite successful in cell 2 (nonroutine), but be a waste of time in cell 4. To cite a final example: We have noted that organizations may attempt to move into cell 4 by reducing the number of exceptions that may occur, by decreasing the variability of raw materials, and by finding analyzable ways of solving their problems. However, this victory may be short-lived. If the market suddenly changes, or the technology changes, such an organization may find itself back in cells 3, 2, or 1. It would be well to be prepared to change the organizational structure when such events occur.

More important than the specific examples or recommendations, however, is the perspective illustrated here. This view holds that organizations are not all alike and that the way in which they may vary is in terms of their technology. Two aspects of technology—exceptions and search—are abstracted and analyzed independently and concurrently. Whether or not the scheme just presented is verified by empirical research, and whether or not it proves to have predictive value, matters less than this: before an organization's problems can be solved, it is essential to determine the nature of the organization. Once the determination is made, some administrative and management proverbs may apply very well but others may be irrelevant or even invalid.

The social-structure view of organizations is only beginning to generate such perspectives. To add to the few now current, many more will probably develop in time. Any two may have a compelling logic in themselves but may not be compatible with each other. This should not cause great alarm, since an organization can generally be viewed from several quite different viewpoints or positions and each can yield some useful truths.

The Woodward model. For example, the first major attempt to apply a technological perspective to organizations differs in several respects from the one just outlined but is quite viable in its own right. In addition, it touches upon some important practical matters not covered by the previous scheme. Joan Woodward (38), working at the time out of a technical college in South Essex, England, conducted a study of 100 firms in an industrial area in attempting to test the utility of "classical management theory." She was interested in such matters as ideas concerning types of organizational structure (functional, line, or line-staff); degree of specialization of functions; the optimum span of control and number of hierarchical levels; and staff-worker ratios. None of these factors had any particular significance in relation to organizational success. As she says, this was a disconcerting finding for a group attempting to teach management principles in a technical college. Only after the firms were grouped according to their typical mode of production did the data fall into place. In its most simplified form she uses three types of production systems: unit and small-batch (e.g., made-to-order items, such as custom suits, prototype electronic equipment, custom furniture, and machine tools), large-batch assembly, and mass production (e.g., large bakeries, mass-produced clothing, industrial equipment, autos), and process production (e.g., oil, chemicals, and pharmaceuticals). Simply stated, the three systems may be called unit, mass, and process. She describes the whole scale as roughly equivalent to increasing technical complexity, or technical advance in historical terms.

Considered in this way it appeared that firms with similar production systems had similar organizational structures—despite the variety of products involved. . . .

. . . The critical function is different for each type of organization. Unit firms tend to be dominated by engineering personnel; mass-production firms by production people; process firms by marketers. Similarly, the relationships between these groups, the amounts and kinds of stresses, the difficulties of integration and cooperation vary in rather complex ways in each type. But the most important conclusion is that there is no evidence to prove that sales, production, or development is most important in all organizations. The importance of a function depends upon the specific technology employed.

With a comparative perspective like this, which shows that there is no "one best way" of doing things in all organizations, many well-accepted and even commonplace generalizations are challenged. Instead of applying to all or most cases, such generalizations hold true only for specific types, as we have just seen in terms of the importance of sales or production. . . .

Only when we began to look at the differences between organizations and to categorize them in some meaningful way, such as by technology (though there are undoubtedly other ways), can we begin selectively to apply the multitude of insights offered by organizational analysis.

Footnotes

[1]For technical articles discussing these ideas see Perrow (21, 22, 23).
[2]For example, see Bennis (3), McGregor (19), Likert (17), Gouldner (12), Crozier (6), and V. Thompson (36).

8 "Integrative" Organization Theory

● The focus of Ralph Stogdill's work is individual behavior and group achievement. His theoretical formulation is drawn from the analysis of a large number of empirical research efforts dealing with individual, group, and organization variables as well as previous theoretical developments in groups and organizations.

Stogdill describes multiple outcomes of organizations. While others have recognized, at least implicitly, that the result of organized behavior is certainly something more than some particular product or service, Stogdill's treatment is somewhat different from those of others. For example, Argyris (1) suggests that the evaluation of organizational effectiveness should be determined in terms of the energy required to carry out the three core activities in relation to their pay-offs. These activities are achievement of the objective, internal maintenance, and environmental adaption. But, unlike others, Stogdill has postulated relationships between these outcomes. He suggests what might happen to responsiveness and integration, outcome variables along with productivity, when there are efforts to increase productivity. And this is an important point, not because his statements of the relationships are necessarily correct, but rather because they represent hypotheses of a nature that are rarely advanced in organization literature. They suggest not only that trade-offs are important, but also the nature of these trade-offs when pressures are increased.

Second, Stogdill's concept of structure, one of his intervening variables, provides several interesting considerations in the manner in which it is related to the output variables. He postulates curvilinear relationships between structure and outputs. High structure is ineffective, but then so is low structure. Notice, however, that these relationships are moderated by the nature of the work and the satisfaction of the members of the organization.

Stogdill's work is included here because it seems to be an approach which can accommodate some of the many different points of view presented earlier in this book. Stogdill acknowledges the impact of formal organization structure on behavior. On the other hand, he provides a set of concepts to deal with the problem of how individuals may alter the structure system. Thus, to use the terminology which Scott (29) attributes to the neoclassical school, formal and informal organizations, Stogdill provides a way of considering how both these aspects of organization interact to yield stable behavior patterns.—H.L.T.

A Summary of Stogdill's Theory of Individual Behavior and Group Achievement

ALAN FILLEY AND ROBERT HOUSE

In 1959 Stogdill published *Individual Behavior and Group Achievement* (33), a book which may prove to be a major contribution to the field of organization theory. It contains a theoretical model of organization behavior which synthesizes and explains the results of some 800 research studies. The theory was developed by identifying the elements of organizational behavior found in the research studies and manipulating these elements until an internally logical, predictive system emerged.

We believe the theory to be important for several reasons:

1) It resolves much of the apparent conflict and confusion between researchers and theorists who have stressed structural-functional aspects of organization and those who have emphasized behavioral aspects.

2) It offers an explanation, inferred from social science and business research findings, of (a) the relationship between organizational, group and individual objectives; (b) the interaction between formal and informal organizational behavior; and (c) the multidimensional aspects of group achievement.

3) The breadth and empirical orientation of the theory provide a basis for integrative research including several schools of thought.

Throughout his theory, Stogdill attempts to preserve internal consistency of meaning and logic and external agreement with available research. To understand its contents completely, one should follow the precise definitions of terms used in the original work and carefully read Stogdill's review of the research cited to support the theory. However, for present purposes a simple and nontechnical summary, with examples, is presented. The authors have occasionally taken the liberty of retitling some of the critical variables for clearer understanding. Certain relationships that are implicit in the original work are made explicit in this summary. These changes bring the inevitable risks of misinterpretation, omission, and misemphasis, for which the authors must be responsible. In general, however, every effort was made to preserve the wording, essential variables, and intent of Stogdill's theory in the summary which follows.

Thanks are due the publisher and Dr. Ralph M. Stogdill for permission to use the ideas and concepts presented in *Individual Behavior and Group Achievement* (New York: Oxford University Press, 1959). Special thanks to Alan C. Filley and Robert House for their permission to use the summary they prepared.

The theory

The theoretical model is based upon nine variables which are classified into three groups: input, intervening, and output variables, as here:

Input Variables	*Intervening Variables*	*Output Variables*
Member interaction	Member satisfaction	Group responsiveness
Individual performance	Group structure	Productivity
Individual expectation	Task-oriented work	Integration

The *input variables* are (a) member interactions, (b) individual performances, and (c) individual expectations. *Intervening variables* are (a) member satisfaction, (b) group structure, and (c) task-oriented work. Intervening variables follow inputs in time, condition input variables, and are partial determinants of group achievement. *Output variables* (describing group achievement) are (a) productivity, (b) integration (cohesiveness), and (c) responsiveness (drive).

Input variables. Interaction is defined as an action-reaction sequence in which the reaction of any member in a group is a response to the reaction of another member. Thus, where interaction takes place there is a mutual reaction between two parties in the group. It is necessary to distinguish between simple reaction and the more complex interaction. Reaction is a one-way process which may be represented by the statement "A responds to B," whereas interaction is a two-way process which involves both A's response to B and a reaction by B to A's response.

Stogdill defines a *group* as an open interaction system in which actions (or reactions) determine the structure of the system and successive interactions exert equal effects upon the identity of the system; that is, the group retains its identity and continuity even though individual members may enter or leave. The group evidences structure through the predictable actions or reactions of group members. As we shall see later, the extent to which predictable behavior is possible in group members determines the freedom of each of the members.

Group members contribute both performance and expectation to the interaction system. *Performance* is defined as one of the actions or reactions that constitute the task-oriented work of an interaction system. It is an action which identifies an individual as a member of group operations. The actor saying his lines, the lathe operator running his machine, or the manager planning work of subordinates are all exhibiting performances which identify them. Differences in performance provide the basis for differentiation of structure in groups and may be influenced by external or internal factors such as intelligence, special aptitudes, length of the working day, lighting, pacing of work, etc. Some 60 years of human engineering research has increased performance by matching the proper man to the job under proper conditions.

The expectation of group members is also an important contributing factor in the interaction system. Management students are well aware of the effect of attitudes in increasing or decreasing group performance. Stogdill defines *individual expectation* as readiness for reinforcement, and says that expectation is a function of (a) drive (level of tension or reactivity exhibited by an organism), (b) the estimated probability of the occurrence of a possible outcome, and (c) the estimated desirability of the outcome. The estimates of desirability and probability may also reinforce each other if operating in the same direction and lowered probability may diminish desirability estimates. Also, probability estimates tend to be overestimated when the expected outcome is desirable (positively valued) and underestimated when the expected outcome is undesirable (negatively valued).

Probability and desirability estimates differ not only in kind but in rate of change as well. Estimated desirability rises rapidly toward its maximum value in response to initial reinforcement, and further reinforcements exert a diminishing amount of increase in desirability estimates. Estimates of probability, on the other hand, tend to rise more slowly.

Thus, one may infer that in situations where desirable group goals have been provided, perceived confirmation (reinforcement) of the likelihood of attaining these goals will elicit initial group support even if the goals actually prove to be improbable. Similarly, an individual's motivation may be regarded as a function of his drive and of the confirmation of his desirability estimates.

The group may also act upon the expectations of a member, causing him to adjust his values to the group norms or to reject the group in favor of values more suitable to him. Conformity to group norms is facilitated when the members are strongly motivated to remain in the group, when they desire group reinforcement of their own value systems, and when the group norms are clearly defined; conformity is also facilitated when the group members have access to accurate information about the norms, when the group is more highly valued by the individual than other reference groups with conflicting values, and when the group is able to reinforce expectations.

The extent to which group norms work for or against formal organization goals is strongly influenced by intervening variables, particularly that of structure.

Intervening variables. The intervening variables of the Stogdill model influence the effectiveness with which inputs can result in a satisfactory group achievement.

The first and most important intervening variable is group structure. This variable has for a long time been recognized as a critical factor in attaining successful group action. Stogdill defines *group structure* as the differential regularities of action and reaction exhibited in the positions in a system. The position of a group member exhibits predictable patterns of performance. Group members perceive these patterns and thus confirm probability estimates of each other's performance.

In other words, the position of a member in an interaction system is defined by predictability of action and reaction. This predictability operates as a stimulus to predictable reaction by other members of a system. Thus, once structure is established and action by group members becomes predictable, then members can act upon that predictability without relying upon continuous interaction, such as checking with others for information, obtaining approval, etc. The optimum degree of structure confirms the group interaction pattern and permits the successful accomplishment of group goals, whereas less of more than optimum structure may seriously restrict group output.

A structured system thus permits members freedom. *It increases the area of freedom for its members* because the predictable individual differences in performance which define the positions in the system permit areas of action which are *not* responses to the actions of other members.

Individual freedom is highest under moderate degrees of structure. If one understands the basic doctrine and values of an organization, is allowed to interpret each situation in the light of these values, and can take discretionary action within predetermined limits, his area of freedom is both clarified and enlarged.

Individual freedom is at a minimum under extremes of high or low group structure. When group structure is too high, the individual is controlled by the system; when too low, the individual must rely upon constant interaction. If, for example, one's job is rigidly defined by repetition, procedure, or established practices, he has little freedom to act. If, on the other hand, each time one takes action he must get a new definition of policy or authority from his superior, he also has little freedom to act. This curvilinear relationship between freedom and structure is supported by a number of research studies and serves as an important link between the structural-functional school and the behavioral school of management scholars.

Group structure is composed of two subsystems, a position system and a role system. The *position system* is the more permanent of the two. It is organized by status (levels) and function (work activities). *Status* is defined as the degree of freedom granted the occupant of a position in initiating and maintaining the goal direction and structure of the system. *Function* is the general nature of the contribution that the occupant of a position is expected to make toward the accomplishment of a group purpose; this definition is analogous to the concept of general work assignment familiar to students of functional management. Both status and function create a hierarchy of positions referred to as the formal organization. Once it is established, the formal organization is quite stable; the status and function of a position remain rather fixed even though the occupant of the position may change.

The second subsystem of structure is the *role system*. The role system is an expected pattern of behavior that is attached to a person rather than to the position which he occupies. Two members holding the same position may be expected to perform different roles; for instance, the subordinates of two foremen with similar status and function may expect different patterns of leader behavior from each. Expectations by group members concerning a member role are influenced by three factors: the nature of the position itself, member demands brought on by changes in structural and operational requirements, and a member's perception of the kind of person that he is.

The role system is an informal structure that is less permanent than the position system. It is defined by authority and responsibility. *Authority,* as used here, is defined as the degree of freedom that the occupant of a position is expected to exercise in initiating performance and interaction within a formally acknowledged structure. *Responsibility* is the set or range of performances that a member is expected to exhibit by virtue of the operational demands made upon his position in a formally acknowledged structure. It should be noted that while status and function in the formal position system and authority and responsibility in the role system are parallel concepts, they are not necessarily equal.[1]

Both the position and the role structure are determined by group interaction in the absence of any formally established relationships. When the formal organization is defined by management, however, it is adjusted to meet the needs of the role structure; the role structure adjusts to it, or both. As group members interact, their individual expectations are either confirmed and reinforced or they are not confirmed. When confirmation and reinforcement occur, a pattern of relationships is defined between members in terms of performances and expectations. If the pattern meets with the approval of group members, it is translated into a structure which defines the individual position and role of each member as related to the group purpose.

When structural patterns do not meet with member approval, adjustment is necessary if an acceptable structure is to be developed. Resolution of the conflict takes place through the interaction process. Sources of conflict are many and varied; subgroups may have conflicting goals; subgroups may expect different roles from the same position (for example, a foreman may be viewed differently by management and by his own subordinates); or role expectations may differ from position expectations.

Suitable group structure is also prerequisite to an optimum degree of the other two intervening variables, member satisfaction and task-oriented work.

Member satisfaction may be defined as the sense of personal well-being one feels when his goals or expectations are being met. (This definition is implicit in the theory.) The accomplishment of personal goals may or may not lead to the accomplishment of production goals of the formal organization. Nor does it necessarily follow that satisfied individuals create a group that is responsive to continued change and development. It is clear, however, that individual satisfaction bears a curvilinear relationship to structure; that is, satisfaction is most likely to be highest under intermediate degrees of structure. Unless a member knows what is expected of him by other members of the group and how well he is meeting these expectations, he is not apt to be satisfied with his own performance or with the performance of other members of the group.

Task-oriented work also bears a curvilinear relationship to structure.[2] *Task-oriented work* is defined as all of the actions and reactions which maintain the structure and accomplish the purposes of the group. Member performances which are not directed toward group goal attainment or maintenance of the group structure are not considered part of this task-oriented work; that is, sleeping, reading, or having one's hair cut on company time (if not job connected) would meet personal but not group goals. As might be expected, task-oriented work is positively related to the achievement of total group productivity.

The relationship between the intervening variables and the various kinds of group achievement will be explained in the discussion which follows.

Types of group achievement. Group achievement (output) may be defined as the sum of the outcomes experienced by the group as a result of interrelated performances, interactions, and expectations of its members, as affected by intervening variables. It is essential to recognize at the outset that the output of the group is divided among three factors: productivity, responsiveness, and integration. It is not solely productivity.

Stogdill emphasizes that he has not found it possible to construct a logically consistent theory based on the hypothesis that productivity is the only achievement of organization. Rather, the achievement of an organization is divided among the three types of output.

The first of the outputs, *productivity*, is defined as the degree of change in expectancy values created by task-oriented work. Productivity measures the values created by the members for the group. While clear measures have yet to be found, productivity is generally measured in industrial organizations in terms of dollar value of output compared with dollar value of input.

Subgroups tend to develop norms which regulate productive output at a rate that is comfortable for their average members. The total group will establish a standard of productivity that can be fulfilled by all of its subgroups. For example, financial incentives have only short-term effects where they are based on quotas which are above group norms.

More lasting effects upon productivity are achieved by permitting the members of lower-status positions to have role boundaries that enlarge their responsibility and authority. People tend to perform near the outer limits of their roles because they derive pride and satisfaction from demonstrating their competence to meet the expectations of others. When roles are sufficiently large, therefore, group norms are elevated to accommodate the defined area of responsibility and authority. Management literature contains many instances where job enlargement has provided an opportunity for increased responsibility and authority, resulting in positive changes in productivity and job satisfaction.

Productivity bears a curvilinear relationship to structure. It is normally highest under intermediate degrees of structure.

Structure is also curvilinearly related to another measure of achievement, responsiveness. *Group responsiveness* (drive) is defined as freedom from restraint in action toward a goal.[3] Freedom to act, freedom to interact, and freedom to reinforce expectations are examples of group responsiveness.

The responsiveness of a group may be too high or too low. If too high, as Stogdill points out, a military group may be destroyed by its willingness to charge wildly into withering enemy fire; if too low, it will fail to attack at all.

Continued favorable responsiveness is, in part, a product of success. As the group receives reinforcement of its goal expectations, it increases its responsiveness to further action. Since responsiveness is a function of structure and control, it is also closely related to group leadership.

Responsiveness is not the same as motivation. Motivation is a function of drive and confirmed desirability estimates. It provides the potential for responsiveness, which may or may not be realized, depending upon mediating factors. An individual or group may be highly motivated, yet unable to act. If motivation is to result in responsiveness, there must be attainable goal expectations, a reinforcement of those expectations by experiences of success, the necessary freedom to act, and the proper degree of structure and control.

Group integration (cohesiveness), the third output, is either positively or negatively related to the output of responsiveness. *Integration,* defined as the ability of the group to maintain structure and function under stress, meets the group's needs for structural stability, coordination, unity, and loyalty. An integrated group is characterized as having viscidity; in other words, group members function as a unit and are free from dissension, conflicting interests, and disrupting forces.

Integration is a function of intermember unity and coordination in the support of group structure, operations, and goals. It is dependent upon a clearly defined role structure that is free from role confusion and role conflict; for such conflict typically reduces the value of group membership to the members, the ability of a member to act decisively and his satisfaction with the organization.

Individual satisfaction, an intervening variable, is more highly related to group integration than to productivity and responsiveness. Reinforcement of individual expectations concerning group membership simply confirms the individual's estimate of the value of membership in the group, as well as his probability estimate of experiencing further satisfaction from continued group membership. The effect of satisfying a member's expectations is to increase his support of the group, thus encouraging greater integration.

Individual satisfaction is not the same as integration, however. A group may have highly satisfied individuals but low integration if individuals are idle, playing, wasting resources, or undermining the status structure of the group. Individual satisfaction contributes to group integration only when the reinforcement of the members' expectations leads them to support the group structure, teamwork, and goals.

While member satisfaction is generally positively related to group integration, satisfaction is *not* found to be highly related to group productivity. In fact, satisfaction measures and productivity measures are found more often than not to be negatively related. This relationship is explained by the fact that satisfying experiences, such as talking to one's fellow worker or filing a grievance are often conducted at the expense of productivity. Only when meeting productivity goals is also satisfying are satisfaction and group productivity positively related. Similarly, efforts to build group integration usually takes time and resources which could otherwise be devoted to productivity.

The most frequently observed relationships between the three factors of group achievement may be summarized by the following hypotheses:

1) Productivity and responsiveness are positively related.

2) Responsiveness may be positively or negatively related to integration.

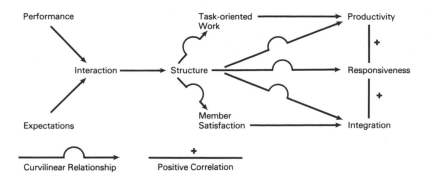

**Figure 1. Group Achievement
when Work Is Satisfying**

3) Integration and productivity are negatively related.

4) Productivity, responsiveness, and integration may be positively related when the group is strongly motivated in striving toward goal achievement (when inputs increase) or when motivation is very low (when inputs decrease).[4]

The organization which is successful in realizing group achievement is one which maintains a *balance of output* between the three factors mentioned. A portion of the input is used in meeting present goals; another portion is expended in maintaining the viability and responsiveness of the group so that future goals may also be reached. Only if inputs increase, may all outputs be increased. Otherwise, one output may be increased at a cost of one or both of the other outputs. High or low amounts of structure and control decrease the effectiveness of performances. When structure is moderate, performances are channeled directly toward task and goal accomplishments, and group achievement is highest.

The relations between output and the other variables in the Stogdill model may be illustrated by considering two typical situations: in the first (fig. 1), work is satisfying and structure and leadership complement each other; in the second (fig. 2), work is dissatisfying and unpleasant conditions are frustrating or stress-producing.

Figure 1 illustrates the first situation. High expectations of goal achievement are supported by positive leadership patterns and structure. Group goals are defined, positions and roles are clarified, job relationships are known and accepted, and policies are stated and accepted. Reinforcement of expectations leads to individual satisfaction of group members, high motivation, and a high level of task-oriented work. The end result is a high level of achievement and a favorable balance between the outputs of the group.

The second situation is shown in figure 2. Here, members have adequate freedom of status and authority, but they find the work itself to be unpleasant, frustrating, or tension-producing. Under such conditions, members may evidence a high degree of group integration associated with

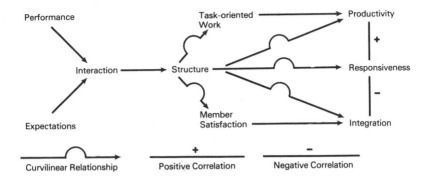

Figure 2. Group Achievement when Work Is Dissatisfying, or Unpleasant, or Conditions Are Frustrating or Stress-producing

low levels of productivity and responsiveness. If these conditions persist, inputs will also be reduced through feedback, causing all group achievement to suffer.

To illustrate the situation shown in figure 2:

> In January, 1962, British postal workers, upset by the government's anti-inflationary ban on wage increases for public employees, nearly strangled the country's postal system. The employees already earned 3.5 percent less than industrial employees and with the ban found their attempts to improve earnings frustrated.
>
> The postal employees reacted to this frustration by a unified move to work strictly by the rule book. By common consent of both the formal and informal organization, rules had not been interpreted literally prior to the government order, yet after the ban productivity dropped precipitously when postmen refused to carry more than the regulation 35-pound load on rounds, refused to leave mail when there was no mailbox, and returned "incorrectly" addressed letters that lacked postal zone numbers.
>
> The members had become more integrated in response to the situation diverting freedom of status and authority toward only one aspect of achievement.[5]

Before the government ban, there was freedom of action which permitted the achievement of both subgroup and formal goals. After their subgroup goals were frustrated, workgroups became more highly integrated and used literal interpretation of workrules as a means of restricting productivity and responsiveness toward organizational goals.

In summary, leadership which strives only for maximum production is overlooking two important elements: responsiveness and integration. Stogdill's theory emphasizes that a leader must seek the optimum balance of group achievement among all three outputs. Undue emphasis upon productivity, if it reduces expectations and integration, may have the effect of actually deteriorating the structure of the group and, therefore, its capacity for future productivity.

Implications of the theory for the field of management

Provides a basis of reconciliation between behavioralists and structural-functionalists. Now that a summary of Stogdill's theory has been presented, let us consider some of its implications for the field of management. One of the most important contributions is its reconciliation of much of the current controversy between the structural-functional and behavioral schools of thought. The functional school has traditionally emphasized formalization of group objectives and relationships through rational policies, procedures, instructions, job definitions, organization structure, and control systems. This school postulates that group achievement relies heavily upon the performance of legalized or appointed functions. These functions are usually classified as planning, organizing, and controlling. The functional school also states that after the group reaches a certain level of complexity, the absence of formalization will result in confusion and ineffective methods of achievement.

In contrast with the structural-functional emphasis, the behavioral school has emphasized the complexities and interrelationships of emotional human beings operating within a viable group system. The behavioralists argue that the functional theory is primarily a mechanical explanation of organized behavior, suffering from the invalid assumption of an economic, rational man. They believe that in assuming complete rationality and overlooking the consequences of emotional and social choice, the functional theorist disregards many essential variables of organized behavior. Some behavioral scientists even imply that the very presence of formal structure will have unhealthy effects on an individual's personality development and, therefore, inhibit the attainment of group objectives.

Both schools show the bias of their origins and early training in their research designs. The functional school emphasizes the standardization, description, and measurememt customary to engineering; the behavioralist stresses variations in value, perception, and choice in keeping with his psychological or sociological background. The functionalist searches primarily for determinants of efficiency; the behavioralist looks for determinants of member satisfaction. Yet both frequently identify different effects of the same independent or dependent variables; for example, the rational aspects of policy formulation versus its social or psychological consequences.

Considering the differences in taste and method of the two schools, it seems that most of their findings are noncomparable, rather than contradictory. For example, the economic value of formal organization is not disproved by proving that group members show sociometric preference or that formal organization forces members to achieve personal satisfactions (and perhaps even self-realization) off the job rather than as part of the job. Only when such effects impede the accomplishment of the organizational objectives do they raise questions of validity concerning formal organizational theory. Similarly, the importance of social systems is not negated by proving the importance of formal organization in meeting business objectives. Unfortunately, this type of inference is found in the literature of both schools of thought.

The hope for reconciliation of the two schools seems to lie in theoretical and empirical work which integrates organizational and behavioral variables into a single system.[6] Stogdill's theory is designed to accomplish this objective.

Stogdill's theory is not only logically structured; it derives its hypotheses from empirical evidence from social science literature in general, including business literature. Stogdill, a social psychologist of note, demonstrates a thorough knowledge of functional theory and research, as well as behavioral. He is one of the few organizational theorists trained in the behavioral sciences who is free from the criticism that he lacks understanding of the classical management viewpoint.

Explains relationships between leader behavior, management functions and informal organization. Stogdill also makes an important contribution to management theory when he shows that the ideal leader behavior is one which succeeds in harmonizing individual expectations and organizational objectives by reinforcing desired member behavior and by encouraging or withholding confirmation of member expectations. Ideal managerial behavior requires the performance of management functions (planning, organizing, and controlling) which provide needed structure to group members. When this structure is absent, members operate under conditions of uncertainty. If structure is properly organized, it provides the necessary basis for realization of expectations and allows members to make decisions and exercise initiative.

The freedom provided by formal structure is an important factor in providing concomitant informal activities which contribute to both productivity and individual satisfaction. This relationship is supported by research which shows that when individual and organizational objectives are harmonious, informal activity facilitates attainment of formal objectives. Informal interaction and formal structure, therefore, can be mutually supportive and provide benefits to both the individual and the organization. It follows that maximum benefit is obtained when both the formal and the informal structure are gradually and continually modified according to desirable patterns of interaction.

Although the presence and importance of the formal and informal organizations are not new concepts to management students, the combination of the two by Stogdill, bringing out their role as mediators of interaction and expectations, provides a way to view organization behavior.

Reconciles apparent contradictions in empiric research. The theory is also important in its explanation of the relationship between member satisfaction and group productivity. It illustrates why behavioral research has shown that member satisfaction and productivity do not necessarily vary positively. It also explains the conditions under which positive and negative variances can be predicted. Relating satisfaction to integration, Stogdill shows that while integration may impede the attainment of short-run productivity, it is necessary for the achievement of long-range business objectives. The sharing of output between productivity and integration is necessary in order to provide a viable, unified group capable of continued effort under conditions of threat or stress. This relationship has important implications for organizations operating under conditions of change, external threat, or internal frustration.

It should also be noted that productivity, integration, and individual satisfaction can receive the best effects of inputs at intermediate degrees of structure. Too little or too much structure will restrict group achievement; this fact should be considered both by those who seek to avoid the definition of structure in business organizations and by those who seek to reduce all activities to routine procedure.

Footnotes

1 Stogdill's terms should be used as defined. Some have a different usage from that in general management literature. The distinction between status and authority (as used here) also points up a source of conflict between management theorists today: *status* is the level of freedom prescribed by the formal organization (often called "legal" or "formal authority") while *authority* in the Stogdill model refers to the level of freedom that is acceptable to the group (on a social or political basis) based on the "consent of the governed" rather than formal delegation.

2 The phrase "task-oriented work" was chosen rather than Stogdill's term "operations" in order to clarify the meaning and intent of the variable.

3 Stogdill uses the term "morale" rather than "responsiveness" for this factor. This use of the term is consistent with writings several decades ago, but it is confusing to those who associate "morale" with any one of its many contemporary usages. The term "responsiveness" seems to retain Stogdill's meaning and avoids potential confusion.

4 When these hypotheses are taken together they appear to be anomalous at one point: If responsiveness increases when productivity increases and productivity increases when integration decreases, then responsiveness should increase when integration decreases. Yet Stogdill says that responsiveness may vary positively or negatively with integration. Since the positive relationship is thus not accounted for in this syllogism, the need for research to explain the inconsistency is suggested. Stogdill himself recognizes that exceptions to each of the relationships posited may occur and recommends further investigation to account for these exceptions.

5 "Rebellion by the Rules," *Time,* vol. LXXIX, no. 3 (Jan. 19, 1962), p. 35.

6 For example, the authors are engaged in a study of the relationship between organization and behavior in the research and development divisions of three large manufacturing companies. We are exploring the relationship between such independent variables as number of superiors, organization level, type of work, span of control, attitude flexibility, intelligence, age, education, time with company, and time in job; with such dependent variables as delegation of responsibility, perceived authority, leader behavior, job satisfaction, performance of managerial unit, and degree of role conflict.

References

1. Argyris, C., *Integrating the Individual and the Organization* (New York: Wiley, 1964).
2. Barnard, Chester I., *The Functions of the Executive* (Cambridge, Mass.: Harvard University Press, 1938).
3. Bennis, W., *Changing Organizations* (New York: McGraw-Hill, 1966).
4. Blau, P.M., Hydebrand, W. V., and Stauffer, R.E., "The Structure of Small Bureaucracies," *American Sociological Review,* 31, (1966), 179-91.
5. Burns, T., and Stalker, G. M., *The Management of Innovation* (London: Tavistock, 1961).
6. Crozier, M., *The Bureaucratic Phenomenon* (Chicago: University of Chicago Press, 1964).
7. Cyert, R., and March, J., *A Behavioral Theory of the Firm* (Englewood Cliffs, N.J.: Prentice-Hall, 1963).
8. Davis, Ralph, *The Fundamentals of Top Management* (New York: Harper Brothers Publishers, 1951)
9. Dill, William, R., "Desegregation of Integration? Comments About Contempary Research on Organizations," in Cooper, W. W. et al. (eds.), *New Perspectives in Organization Research* (New York: John Wiley & Sons, 1964).
10. Etzioni, Amitai, *A Comparative Analysis of Complex Organizations* (New York: Free Press, 1961).
11. Galbraith, J.K., *The New Industrial State* (Boston: Houghton Mifflin, 1967).
12. Gouldner, A. W., *Patterns of Industrial Bureaucracy* (New York: The Free Press, 1954).
13. Kaufman, H., *The Forest Ranger: A Study in Administrative Behavior* (Baltimore: The Johns Hopkins Press, 1960).
14. Krupp, Sherman, *Pattern in Organization Analysis: A Critical Examination* (New York: Holt, Rinehart and Winston, 1961).
15. Lawrence, P.R., and Lorsch, J. W., *Organization and Environment* (Cambridge, Mass.: Harvard Univ. Press, 1967).
16. Likert, R., *New Patterns of Management* (New York: McGraw-Hill, 1961).
17. — — — — — —, *The Human Organization* (New York: McGraw-Hill, 1967).
18. March, J., and Simon, H., *Organizations* (New York: Wiley, 1958).
19. McGregor, D., *The Professional Manager* (New York: McGraw-Hill, 1967).
20. McGuire, J., *Theories of Business Behavior* (New York: Prentice Hall, 1964).
21. Perrow, C., "A Framework for the Comparative Analysis of Organizations," *American Sociological Review,* 32 (1967), 194-208.
22. — — — — — —, "Technology and Organizational Structure," *Proceedings of the Nineteenth Annual Meeting of the Industrial Relations Research Association* (Madison, Wis.: 1967), 156-63.
23. — — — — — —, Technology and Structural Changes in Business Firms," in Roberts, B. C. (ed.), *Industrial Relations: Contemporary Issues* (New York: Macmillan, 1968).
24. — — — — — —, *Organizational Analysis: A Sociological Overview* (Belmont, Calif.: Wadsworth Publishing, 1970).
25. Rigby, Paul H., *Conceptual Foundations of Business Research* (New York: John Wiley & Sons, 1965).
26. Rubenstein, Albert H., and Haberstroh, Chadwick, Jr. (eds.), *Some Theories of Organization* (Homewood, Ill.: R. D. Irwin and the Dorsey Press, 1966).
27. Rudner, Richard S., *Philosophy of Social Science* (Englewood Cliffs, N. J.: Prentice-Hall, 1966).
28. Schumpeter, J., *Capitalism, Socialism and Democracy* (New York: Harper, 1942).
29. Scott, William, "Organization Theory: An Overview of Appraisal" *Journal of the Academy of Management,* vol. 4, no. 1, (April 1961), 7-26.
30. Selznick, P., *Leadership in Administration* (New York: Harper, 1957).
31. — — — — — —, *TVA and the Grass Roots* (Berkeley, Calif.: University of Calif. Press, 1949).
32. Stogdill, Ralph M., "Dimensions of Organization Theory" in Thompson, James D., *Approaches to Organizational Design* (Pittsburgh, Pa.: University of Pittsburgh Press, 1966).

33. — — — — — —, *Individual Behavior and Group Achievement* (New York: Oxford University Press, 1959).

34. Thompson, James D., *Organizations in Action* (New York: McGraw-Hill, 1967).

35. Thompson, Victor, *Modern Organizations* (New York: Knopf, 1961).

36. — — — — — —, Bureaucracy and Innovation," *Administrative Science Quarterly,* 10 (1965), 1-20.

37. Weber, M., *The Theory of Social and Economic Organization,* trans. by T. Parsons (New York: The Free Press, 1947).

38. Woodward, J., *Industrial Organization: Theory and Practice* (London: Oxford University Press, 1965).